£2.50

Heavy Rescue Squad Work on the Is[land]
Bill Regan's Diary from the Second [World War]
by
Ann Regan-Atherton

Edited by Mick Lemmerman and Co...

© Ann Regan-Atherton, 2015

FOREWORD

Isle of Dogs Heavy Rescue worker Bill Regan kept detailed, handwritten notes and diaries during World War II, all of which were transcribed by his daughter Ann in the late 1980's. In 2015, the editors – keen Isle of Dogs amateur historians - were fortunate enough to be given access by Ann to the diaries for their research. We were immediately captured by Bill's narrative and Bill the character, and could not help but think his diaries would also be enjoyed by a wider audience. We asked Ann if we could publish the diaries on her behalf and, happily, she enthusiastically agreed.

So, we set about scanning her typed transcription (created at a time when word processors and digital copies were not common) in order to create an editable format from which we created the book you see before you.

In the original transcription, as you would expect, Ann deliberately copied her father's diaries word-for-word, including spelling and other mistakes. In this '2015 edition', we have corrected spelling mistakes and some of the punctuation and grammar (as far as the latter two are concerned, we have tried to keep changes to a minimum in order to retain the rhythm and colour of Bill's words, but some changes were necessary to improve clarity).

Another change in this edition is the inclusion of geographical notes. Bill's diaries make many references to buildings, streets and places on the Isle of Dogs which are now gone and no longer known even to Islanders, unless they are from an older generation. We are convinced that Bill's diaries would also be of interest to readers with no connection at all to the Isle of Dogs, and hope that the notes help them to follow Bill in his rescue operations around 'the Island'.

Bill was also a keen photographer and took many photos of the bomb-damaged local streets (he was risking a prison sentence of up to 3 years for taking such photos; ironically, his photos were developed by a policeman friend of Alf Crawley). Unless otherwise stated, photographs in this book were taken by Bill. Maps were created by Mick Lemmerman.

Finally, Ann has kindly proposed that all proceeds from this book be donated to the Friends of Island History Trust, a charitable organization run by locals who wish to record and preserve the local history of the Isle of Dogs.

Mick Lemmerman, Con Maloney, December 2015.

Original Editor's Note

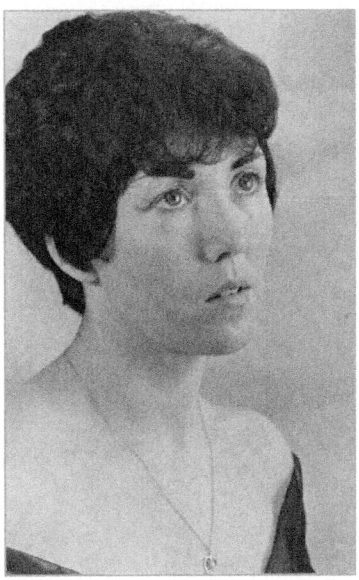

Ann in 1966

In compiling this diary I have made every effort to reproduce the original manuscripts accurately. Many were written under stress, and in the most primitive conditions of life - often with only the aid of a pencil and a candle.

Where words have become indistinct or been omitted I have guessed them from the context, and indicated this with brackets. The occasional spelling and punctuation errors, or words repeated in sequence, have been reproduced exactly. Many of the early transcripts are undated, but my father's memory, plus official verification of some of the air raids, have helped me to place events into a fairly reliable sequence.

I wish to thank the Imperial War Museum for their interest; also Poplar Central Library who gave us access to the officially documented recordings of bombing incidents on the Isle of Dogs. In particular, my thanks to Dr. John Fines for all his practical help and advice, and to my husband for his encouragement and patient assistance with proof reading.

Finally, my thanks to my dear Dad, without whose foresight and diligent recordings, none of this would have been possible.

Ann Regan-Atherton B.A.
October 1989.

Original Preface

Bill and Vi on holiday in Selsey Bill, 1968

In the beginning my interest was to keep an account of my activities during the war against Hitler's Germany; then, in the event of my death or that of my dear wife, the writings would reveal something of ourselves to our two daughters who might derive some comfort from this. Since both we and the diaries survived, I subsequently stored the loose papers and exercise books in a cardboard box and forgot about them.

Eventually, my wife suggested that the space occupied by this rubbish could be used for something more worthy. I read some or the loose leaves, and, deciding they were of no further use, I consigned them to the rubbish bin. I would read the rest later and then discard them also.

One day early in 1985 I was doing this very thing when my youngest daughter Ann paid us a visit. She began to read the scattered papers with great interest, and was quite appalled at the prospect of their imminent destruction. They represented valuable contemporary historical evidence apparently, and as she had recently gained an honours degree in history, I took her word for it.

In due course the scribblings, now dignified by the title of "documents" were collated, copied, typed and verified where possible by my daughter. She then contacted Dr. John Fines, head of the Faculty of History at the West Sussex Institute of Higher Education, who was equally enthusiastic about the stuff. After spending a pleasant weekend with us he wrote the introduction - giving me inflation of the head. He then sent a bound copy to the Imperial War Museum.

The museum requested permission to copy the diary for their archives; it seems it will be of considerable interest to those who visit the museum to study the Home Front during the Second World War. The Department of Documents wish to store the original manuscripts, once the diary has been published. We have decided that this would be at fitting home for them and have agreed.

Fifty years on, my scribblings are finally laid to rest.

William Bernard Regan,
October 1989.

Original Introduction

If you have had little more to go on in forming a picture of 'typical' East Enders than the antics of Alf and Else Garnett then a visit to the household of Mr, and Mrs. W. B. Regan can come as quite a shock to the stereotype. Yes they are unpretentious folk in an environment thick with knick-knacks, they are full of talk and demonstrative, their views are firm even to prejudice, but there the likeness ends, and the substantial difference begins.

Mrs. Regan, a homely and comfortable body called Vi, has a passion for crosswords. So let's have no nonsense about it, she has started on a compendium of all knowledge in neatly tabulated lists. What are American states colloquially named? She has a list. What is the language of herbal lore? Turn to list 27b. It helps with the crosswords enormously, but is taking over her bottom drawer which seems full of manuscripts - what's this one? Oh that's all about Greek legends – I'm very prone to them. Look up what I have to say on Haephaestos, I think I did that rather well. Urn - yes. I have to admit you did, Vi, it is not just correct it is immaculate and very well written. I think there's nothing to beat old Homer, don't you? Well no, now I come to think of it dear. I don't.

Yet this is the lady who spent much of her life dipping her hands in linseed oil, grabbing a rough edged and acid covered tin and scooping up a load of rich black paint on Storer's Wharf. The evening shift of three hours, after a full day's work brought in LI.32, and her chapped and bleeding fingers had to be outside the bedclothes at night because she couldn't bear a blanket's weight. This is the lady who was blown up, lived comfortably next door to unexploded bombs, clamoured to be let off the bus to collect the parachute from a flare laid down to mark the oncoming bombers' tracks, and went out to brave the red hot shrapnel covered only by her mum's large enamel basin (she proved it worked).

How can all this be? I am unnerved - Mr. Regan seems to be Bill to some people some time. Bern to others at other times. I can't work out the distinction, and am certain I don't fit the pattern, so I stick to Bill. And Bill is equally something special. I already know that he writes with quite extraordinary narrative ability - nothing cluttered, direct, simple, pointed and with a power of observation that is clearly backed by outstanding native wit, a wild degree of curiosity and almost perfect total recall. I have read the diary and know that it is good, very good indeed, but how the devil did he and Vi get their correctitude of language - not just grammar, spelling and handwriting, but a natural correctitude that should come from years of practice - which clearly they can't have had.

But hold - it isn't just writing. He is an omnivorous reader (the house filled brimful with books, all read and re-read) and his are literate instincts - the diary comes, astonishingly from borrowing Pepys from the local library (and with a touch of Irish charm he explains in convincing detail why it never got returned - I do understand Mr. R.. yes indeed, there wouldn't have been much demand for it, no) He paints and sketches and photographs with remarkable skill, again self-taught. He wanted to draw those Kentish churches he saw on bicycle rides, so he looked at how they did it in books and noted where he was going wrong. When clearing a bombed out school he found some oil paints, but no books to help, so all that had to be done by trial and error - lots of disasters came from using household varnish, but on we go, learning from mistakes.

How did you learn to play, Bill? By now I could guess the answer that was coming - by watching a player of a one-string fiddle, by watching Mr. Appleton the organist, working it all out, persisting in applied curiosity Same with the anatomy, really, although there was the problem with father and the librarian declaring anatomy books too risqué for boys. With the skill of the streetwise Mr. R, told the librarian his father wanted him to have the books to learn to become a football club trainer and masseur - well you must bend the rules from time to time, if ever so gently.

William Bernard Regan is third generation Irish, and by chance was born in Coventry where his father, a football professional was working at the time. But he, like Mrs. Regan, is firmly of Island stock. It is no job of a total stranger to describe the extraordinary compound of experience and sentiment that adds up to the Isle of Dogs, but some attempt must be made for the reader who like me, a few weeks ago, had only the vaguest idea of where it might be It is the southern tip of the horse-shoe in the Thames, five miles from St Paul's (which remains clearly visible) and bordered on the North by the West India Docks and the bridges on either side of the docks, which turn the Island into what it is, and to the South, through the foot tunnel under the Thames by Greenwich, although the rich complex of seventeenth and eighteenth century buildings there is best seen from the Island Park, hard by George's tea stand.

The Island feels cut off, self-contained, and until the recent attack by the London Docklands Development Corporation, which is converting every inch of river frontage into nasty brick shelters for the intolerably rich, was very much a place for Islanders People did stay there for generations, serving the wharves and docks, working in the many factories devoted to the processing of oil, lead, fruit and iron, and keeping themselves very much to themselves. Apart from the rich excesses of the inhabitants of the Bay (after all, only two streets and usually only drunk and disorderly), the Island kept itself free from crime, pointing the few criminals it produced to the rich pickings to be had elsewhere.

Nor was the Island heavily politicised (though as will be clear from the ensuing diary, every islander knew clearly what was what in political terms.) The community was mixed, overwhelmingly the poor in work, but with a leavening of foremen and managers who, despite their different lifestyle lived cheek by jowl Mr R recalls from the first world war a time when he and his brother developed a deep admiration for some children who came to school barefoot, and one day, unnoticed by mother, they kicked off their boots and socks in the coal hole under the stairs and fled off to school to join the new fashion There to their horror they were met by deep concern and immediately reshod (in shoes!) from anxious parents of the better off.

On the way home they managed to palm off the compromising footwear on a poorer boy, and re-donned their coal smeared socks and boots before going up stairs. All would have gone well if the delighted mother of the recipient of the donated footwear had not called in to say thank you (first belting), and if, on being sent to bed early they had thought to wash the coal-dust from their feet, which spoiled the clean sheets and resulted in a second treatment.

Mr. Regan, like Mrs Regan, left school with recommendations for higher things - clerical work, in faith, central schools and higher learning! They both felt this was beyond them, financially and in the real terms of their daily existence. Interestingly Mrs Regan, forced by the exigencies of war, later found herself in a very responsible clerical position in the Admiralty, directed by lieutenants descended respectively from the composer of Swan Lake and the author of the Water Babies. She seems to have helped them through.

Mr Regan knew what he wanted to do from the start - he would be a bricklayer, and in a five year apprenticeship he used his curiosity, wit and application to become a versatile and successful workman. He can today look on a range of buildings (ending in the Houses of Parliament) in which he had a hand. It was hard work, especially in the winter, when persuading the overseer that it was not freezing when it really was, involved using many tricks, (ranging from holding a mug of tea by the thermometer at a strategic moment to the more extreme course of a quick pee over the mortar), for work had to go on - otherwise there was no pay. He recalls the cracks worn in his forefinger by the wiping off of frozen mortar that enabled him to present his daughters with their sixpences balanced vertically on his outstretched hand - not a happy image, but one which amused the children.

In 1939 there was a call for building workers to join in squads to face the results of bombing. Mr. Regan could recall explosions of the previous war that had covered the beds with glass, but he did not really know what was to come. All he knew was that the instructors who came to teach them detoxification and tunnelling techniques had no idea of how rescue work was to be done. He and his mates, steeplejacks, builders, excavators, knew how things went up, and could guess how they might fall. They had their own tools, and some arm-bands, and an instructor who got in the way. But they were ready, and knew they had to cope somehow. For the Island was home, however it was to be battered, and the only sense was to stay, to shore up what was falling and to dig for those who had been covered.

He decided to keep a record of it all, for his daughters. Perhaps he would not survive, and perhaps the record would. Then they would know and he would have done his job. So he would write what happened - no romance, no fine writing, nothing fancy, just what was happening as it happened, day by day.

Much of the material was lost, but what remains is an important contemporary record of a cataclysm that he refused to let bury him. In writing about it, he mastered it and leaves for us a monument that allows some understanding of that awful time, and how survival happens. Written in the tension of the moment itself, this record shows more than reminiscence ever can - these fragments speak

Dr. John Fines M.A PhD
West Sussex Institute of Higher Education
Bognor Regis, Sussex,
1988.

BILL'S DIARIES PART I - THE BLITZ

In 1939, Bill Regan was carrying out building work in the Houses of Parliament, and knew that war was imminent. He had spent one month installing auxiliary water supplies under the House, and had also worked above the ceiling of the Chamber, where he overheard the Commons debate on the war. He was even present in the Palace Yard when Chamberlain declared war.

Then came the period of the so-called 'phony war', almost a year of relative peace (for civilians in Britain at least), before 7th September 1940, the first day of the Blitz.

Bill was a member of the Heavy Rescue Service. His squad was equipped and trained to deal with bombing incidents where damage was more serious and specialized lifting and excavation equipment was needed. They used their experience to safely demolish collapsing buildings and work out the safest and quickest way to reach those who lay injured beneath damaged buildings. People who had worked before the war as civil engineers, carpenters, plumbers and in other construction jobs were particularly suited for work in the Heavy Rescue Service.

Bill's Heavy Rescue Service Depot was shared with other emergency services at Millwall Central School in Janet St (schools were closed after children had been evacuated in 1939[1]). When the first Luftwaffe bombers appeared in the skies on that sunny Saturday afternoon, Bill was about to put his training into action.

---

[1] Many children returned during the course of the phony war, but most left again when the Blitz started.

No. 2 Squad, B Shift, Heavy Rescue Team. Back row, left to right: George Huscroft, Bob Thomas, Alfie Clarke, Fred Harrison (Leader), Charlie Crawley (Driver). Front row: Bert Freeman, George Jillings, Bill Regan

7th September 1940

Met Bert Freeman on the way to the depot; saw him trying to put out a fire at Mortimer's, the stone masons in Manchester Rd, next to the Stirling mangle works.

Mucked in with him, and after putting out the fire, we went to the Depot, found all four gangs were out to incidents. Whilst talking in the office, a call came from another depot asking for any available men. Me and Bert, although we were not officially on duty, were the only ones free, so off we went by bicycle to Abbots Road.

As we crossed the first bridge, we could see big fires among the warehouses, mainly the West India South and Import docks, and were still being bombed. As we were crossing the High St[1], three bombs fell in quick succession somewhere near, so we decided it was better to investigate, and do what we could, and anyhow, possible survivors needing help, rather than carry on to Abbots Rd, and dig for buried dead.

We found an oil bomb first, blazing in the middle of the road, we decided it was doing no harm, only to the roadway, so we left it and went on to Newby Place, a warden told us nobody was involved in the other two bombs, one had landed in grounds behind the Church, and other in the docks, and as far as we were concerned, was out of bounds.

We found our job in Dunkeld St, off Abbots Rd. There was quite a mess, not much standing for some distance. We found the leader, and he asked us to relieve two of his men. There was little hope of finding survivors, as the brickwork had simply fragmented, and collapsed into a heap of fire rubble, where the roof timbers went I never found out.

We couldn't use picks and shovels, so we handled it, usually with a piece of wood, and our fingers. We were not too keen on putting a pick through someone we were trying to rescue.

Things were getting a bit quieter, and we didn't seem to bother about anything else except the hole we were making.

After a while a warden wandered over, so we asked him what we were supposed to be searching for. He wasn't sure, but there must be somebody underneath, so we kept going.

There were other men about 20 yards away, similarly engaged.

---

[1] Poplar High St.

About a couple of house, these other fellows let out a joyful shout, "We got one here."

Of course it wasn't a survivor, it was a body.

Me and Bert got our non-survivor just as dawn was breaking and the All Clear sounding. He was an elderly man, fully dressed, still sitting in his armchair, but totally embedded in fine plaster and brick rubble.

We could not lift him out, until we had freed him entirely, the stuff was packed almost solid around him. We rescued the armchair undamaged. We never found the leader who put us to work, but another who had taken over, and was indignant about two strangers poking about on his incident. We got our bicycles at the end of the road where we had left them and came away at about 7.00 AM. I found Vi alright, and her Mum and Dad and sister Mick and her children O.K.

Had a cup of tea and to the depot for my 24 hour shift. Out at 8.30 AM. Canton St, and took over from A-Shift.

Landscape re-arranged, and beginning to look like Spain and Poland.

In East India Dock Rd, road not clear yet, rubble, broken furniture, overhead cables, lamp standards, etc. Cleared the site and found no casualties. A-Shift had accounted for all known persons, we had not been told, so perhaps somebody thought we needed blasting.

Just after dark, we heard guns fire in the distance, then the sirens went off. Before they had stopped wailing, they were over us.

The same treatment as yesterday, only difference, it was all in darkness.

HEAVY RESCUE SQUAD WORK ON THE ISLE OF DOGS

The Mudshoot[1] gun site did its stuff, but was pretty futile.

As we understood it, they were popping off with four 3.7's, which sounded rather feeble to us. They were enthusiastic, and I suppose that was something to be thankful for.

A-Team out almost immediately, and a little later we were away, and off the island.

We were busy for 2 to 3 hours, no dead, a couple of dozen people excavated from buried Anderson shelters, a few bumps and scratches among them.

On our way back to the depot, we stopped at two sites; first showed no signs of life, so after a half-hearted poke around some shelters, we found they were empty. The second one yielded a Warden, and a wartime policeman, who told us that everybody had been taken to a rest centre.

You would have to be stone deaf to rest in any kind of centre.

Back at depot, found everything in disorder. Nobody knew who was where, or what they were doing, which was very good from my point of view, because we were going where the trouble was.

First example was a Warden dashing in with news of a U.X.B.[2] at the back of some houses in Gaverick St, and would we get everyone out, and then find the bomb and erect a blast wall around it.

We were there in about ninety seconds, and we dashed in and out of doors, those that were open - those that were shut, got the heavy

---

[1] 'Mudshoot' was the usual spelling at the time.
[2] U.X.B. 7th – 8th September 1940 code no. 103 at 14 Gaverick St.

boot treatment. We had a fair bag in no time at all, and I believe it was the good ladies of St. Mildred's House[1] who took them over.

We had a couple of fellows still hanging around, and one said there was a fellow still in bed in one house, and they couldn't wake him, he was drunk. I asked one of my mates. George Jillings, to come with me. He grinned, and said he'd enjoy tipping a drunk out of bed. I believe he would. We found him in bed, fully dressed, snoring like a pig, and we could not wake him.

We decided to carry out between us, and he was so heavy, we dropped him, twice, so we bundled him back on the bed and went away.

When we got back in the street, I told Bert Freeman we couldn't persuade the fellow to come with us, and Georgie said that he wouldn't even speak to us, and if he couldn't be persuaded, we had no right to force him. So that left everyone satisfied.

The U.X.B. was across the road, in the back of houses, up against the back garden wall. We looked at this 3 foot hole, but we could only see soft earth at the bottom.

Me and Bert had a reluctant scratch at the bottom, and we both felt something solid. That livened us up, and we speedily uncovered a few inches of metal, and just as quickly decided it was a foreign body, most likely the bomb. We had never seen one, but were most eager to believe it was a bomb, and moved smartly away. Fred Harrison, our leader, met us outside in the road, and insisted seeing for himself, so we took him to it, and after pondering for a few moments told us to find material to erect a blast wall round it. Ignorance I can stand, for that is only lack of knowledge, but idiocy is something else, and I boiled; I told him to get stuffed,

---

[1] St. Mildred's House was an Anglican establishment situated behind St. Paul's Church in Westferry Rd.

nobody was in danger, and it could only make a bigger hole, and bomb disposal had been informed, so I was getting out. He threatened to report me, so I said, "What for? Self-preservation?"

Anyhow, we all went back to the depot, and found that incendiaries had set light to the roof of the main building, but it was soon extinguished, then we could see flames in the N.M.U. storage warehouse next door.

Bert was away and over the roof in no time at all and hollering for water.

George and I dragged the school fire hose up to Bert, who had got across to where the fire was, by reaching across to a blown out window, and climbing through, found a sack or something similar, and beating hell out of the flames. When we reached him with the hose, the water came out of it with the force of a wet bootlace, it was quite limp it didn't matter as Bert had already beaten it out.

When we got down, we found the hose had dropped off the water tap.

The canteen was operational, so we had tea, and a cheese sandwich.

The All Clear sounded a little later, then the other two teams arrived back, and we swapped information, and waited to be relieved at 8.00 hours.

Vi later recalled this night in her own notes, where she wrote:

> "After a 'busy' night spent alone in the shelter, emerged around 6.00 AM, dressed, and inspected the living room. The hearth rug was filthy with soot and debris from the chimney, so she took it outside and banged it against the wall. Then, an armoured car full of soldiers rolled up."

Ann, continues, referring to her mother's notes: "A rather handsome, 'posh' captain asked if she could direct them to Gaverick St. Vi did not answer, just shook her head. He asked again. Vi said that she didn't know. The captain explained that he understood and respected her response; civilians had been warned not to give any information to strangers, who could be 'fifth columnists' or spies. But, if he could not locate the U.X.B. in time, there could be a tragedy involving many lives lost.

So, Vi told him, and after thanking her, the captain to a subordinate, "My God, I take my hat off to these people – they've got guts." Whereupon he and his team removed their caps and treated Vi to a smart salute and a huge cheer.

Vi was thrilled and galloped along to her parents and family nearby, who were eating a measly breakfast. As she entered, they looked at her so strangely that it made her laugh. 'Why are you laughing?' they asked. 'Have you seen your faces?' replied Vi. 'Have you seen your own face?' they said. Vi looked in the mirror and discovered that her turban and face were covered in soot – all she could see were the whites of her eyes. 'OH, I look like bleedin' Al Johnson!'"

9th September 1940, 8.00 AM

When I got home, I found Vi was alright, and Jackie Bowers and his wife[1], who had been in the Anderson with her. The rest of our windows had gone, so I spent some time helping Vi to tidy up.

---

[1] The Bowers family lived in the same house as the Regans.

Went along to her mum and dad and had a chin-wag, and he asked me if I had managed to get any sleep, and when we reckoned it up, I found I had none for about 76 hours. U.X.B. exploded 2.00 PM (at Gaverick St).

This evening listened to the radio, just after dark. Radio cut to half power, concussion waves coming down chimney, soon turned to distant gunfire, then the sirens; went to the Anderson.

Fell asleep, but kept waking each time Mudshoot guns went off, or something fell close.

Three bombs, in quick succession, just like close, closer, and we both thought curtains, when the last one came, but it was near, and only shook us up, then a rattling of falling bricks and tiles.

We didn't bother much after this, and we lay on our bunks and drank tea from our flask, and talked about our two children, trying to decide what to get for their Christmas presents.

10th September 1940

The All Clear went, and we just lay for a while, until we heard her dad calling, "You alright Vilie?" To the depot, on duty 8.00 AM. The mobile hospital stationed next door in the swimming bath, will in future, on hearing the siren, go to the Cubitt Town school, in case the bridges were brought down, leaving half the Island isolated.

We were last out tonight, but were not needed. At height of tonight's bother, some of us were in the open, watching shell-bursts in the sky. The Mudshoot guns were giving tongue, we could hear the shells whistling over us, in a westerly direction, and we could see bombers passing by the face of the moon in an easterly direction, quite unopposed.

Oh well, I suppose we will get better with practice. The rest of the night was noisily uneventful, we were not called on. Nos. 3 and 4 were able to cope.

11th September 1940

On the way home, got to Pier St, found a rope across the road, and Auxiliary P.C. Nimmo, mate of mine; said he tried to get Vi to leave, as there was a U.X.B.[1] opposite our house in Dudgeon's gateway. I said I would get her to leave. I found her sweeping up fallen plaster, and dumping it in the road. She showed me the hole where the U.X.B. had gone, and wasn't concerned about it.[2]

---

[1] Not recorded.

[2] Vi and Bill tended not to make too much fuss judging from Bill's diaries, and didn't dwell on the danger. But in one bombing incident Vi was knocked unconscious by a bomb blast. In the morning, when she came too, she discovered that she had bitten through her tongue and that her eardrum was perforated!

Warden Herbie Martin had tried to persuade her and her mum and dad, to take shelter in Saunders Ness School[1], but they declined. Vi said she wasn't afraid of dying, providing she didn't have a lingering death. Surprisingly, this took away the worry I had at the back of my mind while on duty. Her sister has taken her two little ones with her, to her mother-in-law at Ilkeston, in Derbyshire. There are not many people left around now, most have left the Island, wisely, which should make my job easier. Joined Vi's mum. Met some of the gunners from the Mudshoot today. All very young, none of them regulars, gave them tea, and chatted away until dusk, when the sound of distant gun-fire from down river, then the sirens.

The lads were a bit edgy when the noise came closer and Vi's mum asked them if they were on duty, and they said no. When their guns started firing, of course the house began vibrating, and each time this happened, they looked very uneasy, and Vi's dad said he thought they should go back to camp. They went, quick.

They had been very nervous, and they did the sensible thing. Me and Vi said goodnight, and went to our own shelter in the back garden, and surprisingly, had a good night's sleep, several near misses woke us, but were asleep again almost at once. I suppose the noise is becoming familiar, like the ships on the river, on a foggy night, blowing away on their whistles which we became used to, and regarded as normal background noise.

---

[1] Cubitt Town School, Saunders Ness Rd.

Mudchute anti-aircraft crew

12th September 1940

To the depot 8.00 AM. Two squads been out, one to Stewart St, one to West Ferry Rd. Fortunately, few people to get hurt now, if your shelter did not get a direct hit, you were usually O.K.

Couple of warnings before midday, while we were out. We already were beginning to ignore the daytime alerts. We could see them, and if they weren't in a direct line with us. We'd mount up and drive smartly back to the depot. Nights were very different, all of them were after you, personally. We did some salvage work today, in Galbraith St, for people moving out. The Island was beginning to look derelict already.

Back to the depot for dinner, not out this afternoon. So Bracken, Jillings, and I had a wander down Alpha Rd[1], as far as Byng St, in to West Ferry Rd back to Glengall Rd and the depot.

Mudchute anti-aircraft gun with McDougall's flour silo visible in the background.[2]

For all the damage done, there had been very few casualties. Alert as soon as darkness fell. The Mudshoot opened up with their pop-guns, and they have a search-light to play with now.

To Plevna St, we found no casualties, but visited all shelters down one side of the street, by walking through first house we found open, into the back garden, then climbing over the low walls, and down to the end of the street. Most of the shelters were empty, those we found occupied, had nobody hurt, so we soft soaped them with the assurance that bombs never dropped twice in the

---

[1] Renamed Alpha Grove shortly before the outbreak of war.
[2] Photo source unknown

same place, I knew differently, but they took some comfort from it.

Some of our squad had done the other side of the road with the same result, so we went back to the depot. It was past midnight, but although the activity had lessened, we were not called out again.

13th September 1940

Home 8.10 AM. Vi made a pot of tea, I had some bread and dripping, and decided to wash and shave, but all I got from the water tap, was about an eggcup-full. The water was off. I could get annoyed. Electricity had gone also. Jackie Bowers and Maud have left, gone to stay with Maud's mother, so Vi will be on her own when I am on duty.

Dolly Bell came round this evening, stayed till the alert sounded, and shared our shelter till morning. I climbed out of the bottom bunk, straight into knee-deep water; must arrange for other accommodation.

Depot 8.00 AM. Wheedled a cup of tea and a sandwich from Mrs. Warren. Out to relieve A-Shift at Morant St. Back at midday, found A Shift No.2 squad had brought a parrot in, squashed up cage from Samuda St. The cage was straightened out, and the parrot fed, with bacon rind and crusty bread. It was well educated, and after preening itself, it gave a most wonderful recital of obscene language I have ever heard, and the building trade wants some beating. It finished off with two words, repeated very rapidly, "F… Hitler, F… Hitler, F… Hitler." [1] My sentiments exactly.

We have made the school boiler-house the depot shelter, and can now get some nights rest, provided we stay clothed and ready for immediate getaway.

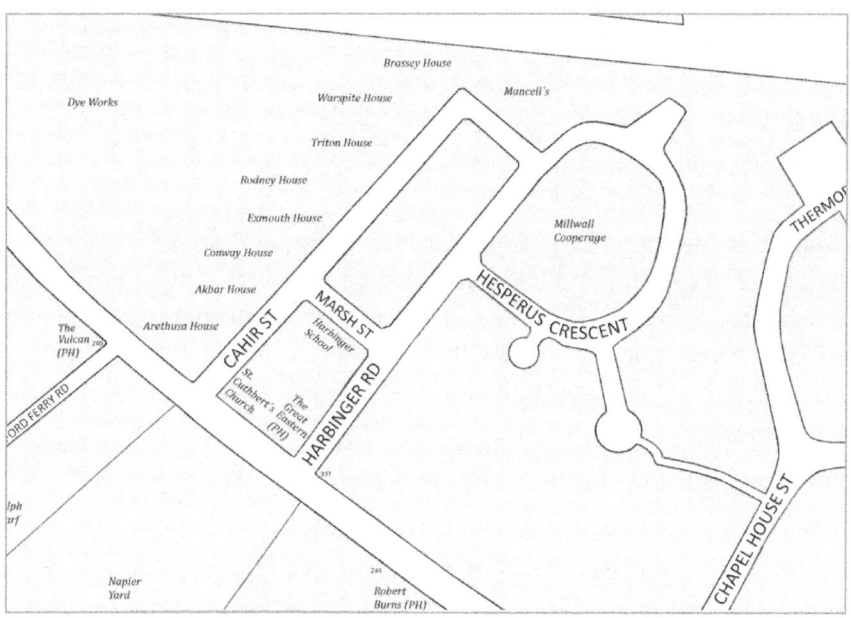

[1] Vi also recalled the parrot from her time working as a volunteer in the canteen, "One day, some 'posh' ladies paid a visit to see how the 'lower sort' were coping. They were very pleasant, and fell in love with the parrot, which, enjoying their attention, entertained them with its Hitler routine." Vi and her mates were horrified, but need not have worried, "The ladies could not understand a word he said, and declared him to be a gallant little chap!" Vi and her mates respectfully agreed, whilst struggling to keep a straight face. Ann was touched that, "as beleaguered as they were, in the midst of chaos and death, people gave their time and hard come by food to bring the little creature back to health – even if he was obscene!"

Tonight, heavy as ever, but were not out until 3.00 AM, to British St[1], no casualties, bomb had fallen in Tyson's Cooperage, right on the dock's boundary fence, so that let us out. Back at depot. Masefield, and Wilkinson's squads were out.

15th September 1940

Home 8 AM, found only one room habitable, shelter still flooded, so Vi has decided to sleep - no, *shelter* - in the front room, with the table pushed beside the fireplace, and mattress and blankets under the table. The window is now heavily boarded, and Vi is confident that she will be safe.

About 10 AM, a mobile canteen came along, and about a dozen of us gathered around and had tea and sandwiches. I didn't know so many people were left along our terrace. This afternoon went to Clary's cycle shop, opposite Christ Church, to buy a bicycle tyre, and found him in army uniform.

He was closing down, so I took the opportunity to buy 2 scooters half price, for the children's Xmas presents.

Not much sleep tonight. At daylight, wandered round through Seyssel St. to Stebondale St. where I found a big gap where several houses should have been[2]. Middle of the crater had been Bill Elderly's[3] house. I knew him very well, so I had a look

---

[1] British St had been renamed Harbinger Rd shortly before the outbreak of war.

[2] Stebondale Street was all but destroyed during the Blitz. Dropping bombs from aircrafts was incredibly inaccurate in 1940 and it is likely that Stebondale Street paid for its proximity to the anti-aircraft battery in the Mudchute.

[3] The Elderlys lived at 137 Stebondale St, just opposite the street's corner with Seyssel St. Four family members were killed Alice, Irene, Bill and Thomas.

around, but only found the remains of the shelter torn out of the ground. No trace of him and his two sisters. I felt depressed. We both belonged to the Dockland Settlement, and in 1930 we had all gone on a camping holiday to Needs Oar Point, near Beaulieu, he and I had spent several late nights with a wireless set, listening to foreign stations, it was like travelling abroad. Later in the week, the coast guards complained that the oscillation from our set was interfering with their equipment, so we stopped our aerial travelling. We had been at school together.

16th September 1940

Depot 8.00, reported to Major Brown about the Elderly's. The night shift had been to the incident but had found nobody. I insisted that they must be somewhere about, maybe injured, so Major Brown came out with my squad to investigate. We gathered three bushel baskets of remains. I picked up two left feet. One of the men saw a body perched on the rooftop. Nobby Clark climbed up and recovered it. It was badly mutilated, it was some time before we were able to identify it as female. I had picked up two left feet, and with a right foot. Major Brown thought the three feet accounted for three people. I said that 2 left and 1 right meant two people. Some of the men were feeling queasy, so rum was dished out. I was T.T., so I gave mine away, and eventually we found enough evidence to account for 3 people, so we came away.

Meanwhile, two squads had been sent for water. They returned with big drums of water, which we took to the canteen for cooking purposes.

One of the Bennetts from Samuda St[1] came for his obscene parrot, which went through its repertoire for the benefit of the canteen

---

[1] At least five adult Bennetts lived at two addresses in Samuda St in 1939: Albert, Edward, Eliza, Frederick and Lilian.

ladies, which includes Vi, who is helping voluntarily. They were scandalized, but still fell around laughing. We are now beginning to notice the smell, as if everything is becoming unclean, not so bad as to be putrid, yet. In the boiler-house shelter, making it more homely. Took Vi home at 4.00 PM, and with her until we heard distant gunfire. I left her under her table shelter, and ran back to the depot before the sirens went.

We were not called out, but spent some time putting out incendiaries. Found a U.X.B.[1] at the top of Mellish St, but nobody in peril, as all homes likely to be affected are deserted.

---

[1] U.X.B. not recorded (first U.X.B. for Mellish Street was recorded 20th-21st September 1940)

17th September 1940

Home, and found Vi had had a worrying time during the night.

A cluster of incendiaries had fallen at the back of the house, and Vi knowing something had landed in the back room, so she went to investigate, and found one had come through the window, and had landed in a tin bath that had clothing that she had washed and ironed, most of them were for the children, and burning, so she had dashed out to the Anderson shelter, and shovelled loose earth into a bucket, and going back and forth throwing it through the window onto the fire until it was out. (I feel rather stuck up with her).

Alert about midday, we saw a fighter plane going across towards Essex, rather high and fast, but the Mudshoot got off one shot at it, and we watched the plane suddenly explode and we were left with a clear sky.

We heard the gunners shouting their heads off. I went round to the site entrance, by the Wesleyan Chapel[1], and the two men on guard were grinning like gargoyles, and all I could get out of them was, "One shot, one bull."

As I came away, one of them said to me, "Wait till we get the four-fives, we'll show them." I hope my guess is right, and that it meant 4.5 A.A, guns. We could do with something a bit bigger, if only to give our morale a lift. The last four nights, we have had a mobile gun on an army lorry, going round the Island, and firing a few rounds in one place, then tearing up the road, a few more rounds, then back again, 'ditto repeato', to cheer us up, or confuse the enemy. Anyhow, it's one of Churchill's better ideas.

---

[1] The Wesleyan Chapel was to the left of the Pier Street entrance to the Mudchute. It did not survive the war.

Our bomb, the U.X.B. under the gateway at Dudgeon's is still there, no-one has bothered about it; perhaps it's been forgotten.

Vi said, "It's quite safe - until it goes off."

That's one cock-eyed way of looking at it.

We are now getting some dirty water through the taps.

Vi's mum and dad are going to Ilkeston today, to daughter Mick at Ilkeston.

Vi's brother Jim, a naval reserve who was called up at the beginning, has had his five children evacuated to Wales. He and Tommy Dann, Mick's husband, are helping to move Vi's mum and dad out, and will accompany them to Ilkeston. Tommy's home town.

Tom, who is a regular soldier, was one of the last away from Dunkirk, and Jim had taken a 'Sun' tug backwards and forwards in the evacuation.

They don't like the night raids, and they have only been here one night. I suppose it is because they must sit and wait, instead of doing something about it.

I hear the subway has had a direct hit[1]. Bomb dropped on the foreshore at low tide, and penetrated the tunnel. Rowing boats from Greenwich are ferrying people across at 2/- a time.

Took Vi to the depot this evening, had a chat with the canteen ladies, and Mr Tyler, who is in charge of A-Shift. Back home at six o'clock, listened to radio, and read from Pepys' Diary. Vi writing letters.

---

[1] Recorded 7th-8th September 1940, High Explosive. When writing 'subway', Bill was referring to the Greenwich Foot Tunnel.

HEAVY RESCUE SQUAD WORK ON THE ISLE OF DOGS

Usual night under the table, nothing fell close enough to worry us.

Depot 8.00 AM. Out at 9.00 to pull down dangerous structures. Back at midday. In the afternoon had a walk round the Island with Bert Forbes.

Saw warden Ernie Lowther this evening, he said most of the people in his area had left the Island, except the male adults who worked on the Island, who seemed to be eating out, and spending the nights in their homes or Andersons.

P.S. These writings were going to be a diary, written at home after each shift, but it hasn't worked out like that. (Silly Me.)

Document 2

Have lost my other writings, will carry on with them as I find time, and paper. Couple of nights ago, we were out before midnight, to Saunders Ness School[1].

What a bloody mess, the whole guts blown away, only the two end flanks standing. There were more than forty people stationed here; I only saw one survivor, the gatekeeper, a man who lived in Pier St, and had lost a leg in 14-18 war.

He said he saw this parachute coming down, and thought it was a barrage balloon, it was a parachute mine, and he was lucky to be on the opposite side to where it landed, with building between him and it. He was blasted into the road, but miraculously none of the debris had hit him. Within minutes we had located the spot they were likely to be, and got two people out, but I don't think they were alive as we were working without lights and they were at best unconscious.

---

[1] Recorded 18th-19th September 1940. High Explosive (but Bill maintains that it was a parachute mine). 27 people were killed, including one man who was not in the school but was standing close by.

I don't know how many we recovered, our relief came on at 8.00 AM, but we carried on until nearly ten, when a squad from the other end of Poplar came to help, so left for the depot.

The victims were fire-brigade personnel, ambulance men, and a complete mobile operating theatre, who were billeted next to our depot, in the swimming baths, and always left for Saunders Ness when the sirens sounded.

Home 10.30 PM, slept on a mattress on the front room floor, until 4.00 PM.

Vi had taken a boat across to Greenwich, and a train to Charlton, to see my mother and younger brother Ken, and sister Dorothy. She got home at 4.30 PM and said she was bewildered by the very little damage there was, compared with the Island. She even had to queue for a tram to get back home. We haven't had a bus for some time.

Listened to the radio, and read for a while, we have water now, so we had tea, two boiled eggs. Mother had given to Vi 'real eggs'. I said to Vi, it reminded me of the condemned man who ate a hearty breakfast. She just said, "Many a true word," and left it at that.

Slept right through until 6.30 AM. Did not hear a thing, I could have been killed without knowing it.

20th September 1940

Both of us to the depot 8.00 AM. Off to relieve at Saunders Ness.

We keep finding bodies, and we are told there were at least 42 to be accounted for, and from what we can gather, there are nearly 2 dozen still here.

Relieved at midday, dinner at depot, back on the job about one o'clock until four.

Nothing exciting tonight. Out once, but only to a site in Stebondale St, as it was empty, it had only been stirred up a bit. The kind of job we like.

21st September 1940

Home 8.00 AM. Vi to canteen. I had a walk round to Saunders Ness, no feverish activity. It's become a depressing routine job. I cannot find any details of the victims, so I don't know if I have lost any personal friends. There is a steel girder, at least fifteen feet long, and 10" from flange to flange, bent in an arc, and the ends pierced the wall of Pinchin-Johnson's, leaving it sticking out like the rail of a theatre balcony.

Most peculiar. On to Newcastle Arms[1], empty now. I went along the passage to the saloon bar, looking at the framed photos of Millwall football team from the early days. I shall try to find some way of acquiring them - legally.

Manuscript Fragment 1. Early September 1940

Last night was a busy one, but different.

There was lots of noise, but none of it seemed to be bombs. High flying bombers were going over from East to West, and there were more than a few.

We had no call-outs, and it was quiet for about a quarter of an hour, so we settled down; a few had made up a card school, and were playing for £1 stakes, the winner to be paid after the war is over.

Charlie Crawley offered to teach me to play chess, but I couldn't concentrate, so finally he and I, Eddie Sullivan and Alfie Clark went outside and wandered round the yard, but this wasn't very productive, and the only suggestion worth any merit came from Eddie, "Get a screwdriver, and open the canteen food cupboard, and brew a pot of tea".

---

[1] Later renamed Waterman's Arms, and now the Great Eastern.

We had liberated the 'makings', when the noise outside started again, so we got back smartly! This lot came from the same direction, but they dropped their loads as they went across. It seemed they were coming in small groups, so while the gun-fire was belting one group, the next group was getting away with it, so eventually, the guns were going off at everything in earshot.

Masefield's party went out, somewhere off the Island, where a bad situation had arisen, and we had had nothing of any consequence, so headquarters had apparently decided to borrow some help from us.

Our turn came next. Davis St, and as we were turning into it, a very shocked warden waved us down, and tried to tell us what had happened and where, but he was in such a state, he couldn't get it out, so our driver, Charlie Crawley, told him to climb on the running board, and point the way.

We finished up at the end of Stewart St, on a derelict bomb site, which had received a direct hit in the middle, and had merely stirred the ruins a bit more.

The warden had apparently been too close, and he had caught the blast, and it had knocked him silly, and he only knows he must get to his post, and phone us, not having recovered enough to realise that nobody had lived on the site for weeks.

We left him at his post, in the care of his mates, and an auxiliary policemen who had come in out of the 'weather', which by now, had got lively.

We made our way down Glengall Rd, but at the bridge, the fire brigade were monopolising the bridge and roadway, so we backed off, went up Farm Rd[1], and on to the depot, and it was the most unenjoyable ride so far.

We were in and out inside five minutes, to the City Arms where a Warden met us, and carted us along to Fletcher's Dry Dock[2]. The only houses along the whole of this stretch of road, from the City Arms to Garford St, are those that were once the houses and offices of the managers of the various firms along here, and are now unoccupied.

[1] The informal name for East Ferry Rd, originating in it being the historic road to/from Chapel House Farm.

[2] Fletcher's shipbuilding company occupied Union Docks on the riverfront north of the City Arms.

That makes two non-events, and I felt cheated. We held a conference, and decided there was no point in searching what was now a ruin, so we started back to the depot, and at the City Arms, Harry King's lot passed us, on his way out, and we threw him a couple of raspberries, which he couldn't hear, and a reverse V sign, which he certainly saw, but didn't appreciate, but we felt a lot better for it.

We stopped at Byng St, and had a few words with Ernie Lowther, who was wandering around. He said something heavy had landed nearby, but he couldn't locate it, because everything around his area looked the same as usual, ruins, but he thinks it was a parachute mine, as he hadn't heard anything approaching, just a big explosion, and he was hoping it had come down on a site that had been bombed previously, which it may well have done, and there are plenty of them to choose. We decided not to hang about, in case we were needed, our luck wouldn't run to three non-events in one nights.

Back at the depot. Bert Freeman went to the office to report, while the rest of us went to the boiler house/cum sleeping quarters, and found the standby squad had made tea, so we joined in.

Minutes later. Bert came from the office. Incident at Galbraith St, volunteers wanted. Bert Forbes. Eddie Sullivan. Sid Packman, George Jillings, Alf Crawley, brother of Charlie our usual driver, and I, took the stand-by lorry, leaving Bert and Charlie tea drinking.

This time, we got to the bridge, driver Alf decided he could get through, which he did, smiling, and taking one hand off the wheel and waving genially a couple of times to a fireman, who wanted us to go back.

Eddie leaned out of the other side of the cab, and bawled at the fireman, "He can't hear you with all this noise, mate, and he's a bit mental with shell-shock."

We carried on to Galbraith St, where we found a warden, two Light Rescue men, with their wagon, and some stretchers.

We spent the next two hours searching, and after shifting enough bricks and timber to build a street of houses, we found nobody.

Just as it was beginning to get light, two fellows came across the back gardens from Plevna St, and had words with the warden, and wandered away.

They were dock workers, and had been using their Anderson shelter for sleeping, and had found a more comfortable one not being used, and had taken it over, and had not told the warden of the change.

The noise had got less now, and was going away, so we lit cigarettes, and decided to walk back to the depot, while Alf bumped the lorry back behind us.

We had no trouble getting over the bridge, the firemen had put the fire out, packed up their toys, and gone home.

When we got back, we found Mrs Warren. Mrs Mack, and Liz Downey, already in the canteen, so we sat around drinking tea until our relief at 8.00 PM.

Manuscript Fragment 2. Early September 1940

…to drop Eddie and I off at the corner of Alpha Rd, and hopefully, we would join up again in the middle of Cheval St.

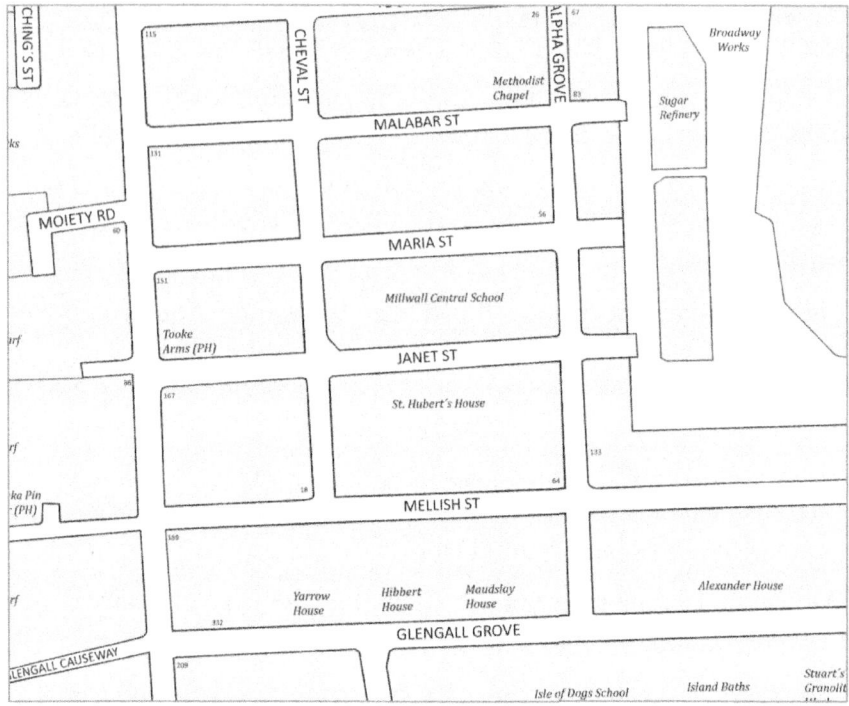

Warden Ernie Lowther met us at Cheval St, said he had nothing definite for us to work on, he having only reported a landmine coming down.

He wisely scrambled for cover, and after it had exploded, came up for air, and found nothing had changed, so concluded it had drifted across Clark's sugar works.

He left us, so Eddie and I worked our way along Cheval St, through the back gardens, found some occupants who seemed to be reasonably happy, which was more than I felt.

I accidently started a small avalanche of brick-work, a large chunk of which landed on my left foot causing me some discomfort that a recital of some of my best swear words seemed to ease.

Eddie had disappeared, the noise much worse and it's lonely, and I wish I had some distraction.

My big toe is hurting again, so I sit on a heap of rubble, take my boot off, and try to re-arrange my sock, so the huge hole in it is away from the sore big toe.

Eddie appears out of the gloom and says, "Found anything young Will?"

I said "No, only a bloody great hole in me sock and a sore toe."

Says Eddie, "That's better than nothing; Alf Crawley and the others are over in Alpha Rd, they've found nothing." And he says, "Should we get back to the depot?"

I thought that was a good idea, and we got across to Alf and the lorry where the others are already aboard.

Me and Eddie get in the cab with Alf, and as we are bumping along. Alf says "Yes, He's got a hole in his sock and it's annoying him."

Alf found this hilarious, and began to shake with silent laughter. Eddie breaks out into his usual chuckle, and I'm giggling, and my toe isn't hurting any more.

Harrison is waiting for us, and before we can dismount, he bawls. "Don't get out, the report can wait, you're the only available squad, get to Strattondale St, there's trouble". We backed out and were away, with cries of indignation from the back of the lorry. When we got to Glengall Rd Bridge, a dock policeman stopped us, said the bridge was unsafe. Alf looked across at me and he says "Well?" I said it looked solid from where I was sitting. Eddie said "Go on Alf mate, take a chance". Alf backs up, the policeman thinks we are going to find another route, and retires to his hideaway, and as he disappears. Alf changes gear to forward and we move smartly across the bridge. As we clear the bridge. Alf stops the lorry and says, "What shall we do now?" On the left of the road a bomb has hit a warehouse and spread a lot of it across the road; too much to drive over.

George Jillings dismounts and surveys the scene, and hears Alf saying something about trying to find another way round. "We can clear away enough of this stuff to get us through quicker than going all round the Island."

We all got stuck in, and in what seemed like minutes, we shifted enough junk to give Alf sufficient road to get us on our way.

As we climbed aboard again, George says to Alf. "There you are old mate, better than going all round the houses."

"Quite right," said Alf, "and I object to being called old." I began to think about Harrison's directive. "There was trouble."

Manuscript Fragment 3. September 1940

…my big toe on my left foot is hurting, the sock has a huge hole in it, we are stumbling around in the dark, and I feel irritable.

We haven't found the warden, so we don't know if he has had it, and as far as we can make out, this area looks the same as it did last visit.

Eddie Sullivan appears out of the same darkness, and says, "Found anyone young Will?"

I said, "No, only a bloody great hole in me sock, and a sore toe."[1]

Says Eddie, "That's better than nothing, anyway. Alf Crawley is over in Alpha Rd, and he says, 'Should we get back to the depot?'" I thought that was a good idea, and we got across to Alf and the lorry, where the other men are already aboard.

Me and Eddie got in the cab with Alf, and as we move off, Alf says, "Anything wrong Bill?" Eddie says. "Yes, he's got a hole in his sock and it's annoying him."

---

[1] Some repetition here; clearly the fragments were different versions of the same story.

Alf found this hilarious, and began to shake with silent laughter. Eddie breaks out into his usual cackle, and when we reach the depot. I'm giggling with them, and my toe has stopped hurting.

Harrison is waiting for us, and before we can dismount, he bawls, "Don't get out, anything to report can wait, you are the only available squad, get to Strattondale St, there's trouble." We backed out, and were away, with cries of indignation from the back of the lorry.

Harrison's illuminating comment that "there was trouble", gave us a wide selection of possible options, none of which filled us with joy.

Anyway, speculation is unproductive, so I stopped thinking and just hoped.

A frantic torch-waver at the off-license corner of Strattondale St, turned out to be a schoolmate of mine. Albert Hubert, now auxiliary P.C., with news that two bombs had come down, one Marshfield St, the other in Strattondale St, on what had been Raggy Turner's rag and bone shop.

The Happy Go Lucky off license on the corner of Glengall Grove and Strattondale St.[1]

[1] Photo: Island History Trust Collection

We dismounted near the library, had a short conference, and decided that George Jillings and Bert Forbes would take the right-hand side of Strattondale St, driver Alf Crawley and Sid Packman to Marshfield St.

Eddie and I started at the first house past the library, the front door of said house lying on the ground, as it had been the last time we were here.

Eddie gave a dirty little chuckle, bent over the door, grabbed the knocker, beat a rat-a-tat with it and bawled, "Anyone home?" and of course, no answer was the stern reply'.

We went through to the back garden, inspecting all the Anderson shelters down to where the new crater was, behind Raggy's place.

We found none were occupied.

We crossed to the Galbraith St, side, repeated the procedure, found two shelters with occupants, the first had a father and adult son, who said to our enquiry, "We are alright mate."

Further on, we thought we had a corpse on our hands, but it sat up, rubbed its eyes, and rather irritably said, "Warrer yer want?"

Eddie asked if he was OK. "Course I am," replied the 'corpse', and went back to sleep.

It was all very depressing.

We moved on, me leading, then I hear Eddie giving tongue, and he is swearing horribly, and he had one foot caught on a length of clothes line.

I helped him get unravelled, and he says, "I thought 'Old Nick' had got me." "No," I said, "he don't go round roping 'em in, he comes up behind, and jabs you up the backside with a big toasting fork, and I don't think he would bother with you, you're too old and tough for toasting. What he's after is a tender morsel like me."

Manuscript Fragment 4. September 1940

We scratched around for a while, but the only interesting thing we found was a colony of cats, as far as we can tell, about eight strong, who scattered when we got too close to them. Eddie and I managed to coax three of them back, and while George Jillings, Packman, Alf Crawley and Bert Forbes continued exploring Marshfield Street, me and Eddie sat on a heap of rubble, and got two of the cats to settle beside us, and after a bit of stroking and ear scratching, they actually began purring, but not the third one, a big ginger, who went sentry-go, backwards and forwards, very unsettled.

Then along comes our lorry, with the rest of the mob on board, and Alf Crawley leans out of his cab, and bawls out, "Livening up a bit Bill, shall we get back?" I hadn't noticed, but it had got heavier and very noisy, with the Mudshoot guns having a right old go, chandeliers floating down, a couple of fires somewhere in West India Docks, and the out-of-step engine noise of the bombers.

It had been a soothing interlude with the poor cats, but everything was back to normal now. We bumped our way back to the depot, where we could see it had been re-arranged. The canteen roof was stripped, the storage tank was pouring water, had a rip down one side, and water was everywhere. The row of toilets nearby, with wooden roofs and doors, was burning furiously. There is a chandelier of flames blazing away on the roof of the Handicrafts Centre - now the offices - and bricks and roof limbers strewn all over the yard.

HEAVY RESCUE SQUAD WORK ON THE ISLE OF DOGS

The depot at Millwall Central School after bombing.

I found old Trice the gatekeeper, wandering round. He seems to be suffering from shock, and is wet through, and except for that he seems to be whole, so I lead him to the boiler-house shelter, get his wet coal and shirt off, wrap a blanket round him and sat him on a bunk. There are people milling around; women and kids seemed to be everywhere. Charlie Crawley was dabbing at a woman's forehead, which was gouged and bleeding, and she is holding hands with a girl about seven years old.

There are two other women seated on a bunk with a couple more children, all a bit scruffy, but appear to be unharmed and not at all worried. Harry King's squad had found them standing around their demolished house, and they didn't want to be rescued, they wanted to get back in their own Anderson shelter. Harry persuaded them to come back with him, and wait for daylight.

I went back outside, it's still noisy, but it's more gun-fire than bombs, and I can hear someone hollering, over by the canteen. It's Eddie Sullivan, and he's kneeling down and he has someone on the ground beside him. It's Kirby, he looks in a bad way, and he's wetter than Trice was. Eddie had heard him moaning, searched around and found him inside the canteen entrance, with water pouring on him from the burst storage tank. I see he has passed-out so I have a feel around and I find his left leg is broken, just above the ankle. Eddie said, "I think his right arm has gone, it's all floppy like." I felt the coat-sleeve and it was all mushy, not like an arm should feel, but his hand is sticking out of the end of his sleeve. "He doesn't weigh 8 stone, Eddie," I said, "so if I carry him in me arms, and you put a hand to the small of me back, we shouldn't aggravate him too much." Just as I lifted him, he opened his eyes and he says, "I think me arm is gone," Eddie had his wits about him, and he lifts Kirby's useless right arm, and said, "Here's your arm, it's alright, you must have fell on it, and you've trapped a nerve, that's why you can't feel it." We got him to the boiler-house and into a bunk, where Charlie Crawley took over.

I went outside again and found Mrs. Warren with her husband's great-coat over the night-clothes, picking her way to the canteen.

We scrambled our way in, and found Bert Forbes and Sid Packman had already cleared up a bit, found the gas to the cooker was still intact, and had already made one pot of tea, so the four of us had a cup, quick, and took the rest of it over to the boiler-house. Activity was dying down, and the first signs of daylight were appearing, so we breathe again.

HEAVY RESCUE SQUAD WORK ON THE ISLE OF DOGS

Bomb damage to the pool at Island Baths, close to the depot at Millwall Central School

Document 3. Christmas 1940

....with my ration of chocolates also, they will have a nice time at Christmas although we will not be there, but we will make up for it after this war is over.

Everyone at the depot has leave owing to them, and as we cannot all take it at the same time, there is quite a bit of bribing going on; but I and Bert Freeman, George Jillings, Bert Forbes, and my driver Alf Crawley have volunteered to stay on over the Christmas period.

Depot 8.00 AM and out to Galbraith St, and Launch St, to retrieve furniture and effects for some people who have found other accommodation further afield. One person was very grateful, and insisted I have her piano, and why I accepted I don't know. I can't play.

Depot at midday, dinner and panic, more victims have been found at Saunders Ness, and we were off at 1.00 PM to relieve.

Found that four firemen had been got out, and signs of more to come.

Bill Barden and his squad stayed on with us and so we spread out, and began searching around in small groups.

After all this time, there is no big stuff to be moved, just one big heap of small rubble and concrete, which has settled into a light mass, and requires hand-work. George Jillings had worked in the building trade with me, and on occasions like this, when it was possible to work in many small groups, instead of one large group, we two tended to drift off on our own, we fitted well together. I had worked on the building of the school, so I knew the general lay-out, and decided we should work down into the long corridor that ran for almost the length of the building. There were no survivors after all this time, 3 months, so systematic clearance is called for. After an hour or so. George called me to help him with a doormat he had found, but could not pull clear. It was black, and of a thick curly texture, so I fished around it for a while, loosening the packed rubble, then George came back with a length of iron rod to prise it out. I told him it was a bloke, and I knew who he was, Warden Herbie Martin.

Meanwhile, everyone else had gathered in one spot, so we went over to find out why.

They had found two, and had sent for the Light Rescue to come and take them away, and while I watched, two more bodies were being uncovered. I know none of us are very happy having to handle corpses, and it shows. They have uncovered 2 young girls, about 18 years of age, quite unmarked, and looked as if they were asleep[1]. I looked around at the other men, and most of them looked shocked, and a bit sick; we had usually found bodies mutilated, and were usually lifted out by hands and feet and quickly got away. Major Brown sees one man being sick, so he fishes out a bottle of rum to be handed round.

By now, I am feeling a bit angry at the prospect of these two girls being lugged by their arms and legs, so I got down beside them, and they have obviously been in bed for the night. They both have only their knickers, and short petticoats on, and dry weather we have had, and the rubble packed round them had preserved them. Their limbs were not even rigid. They were lifelike; I could not let them be handled like the usual corpses. I know I would have belted the first one who handled them with disrespect, but nobody makes a move to shift them, and are just standing there, gawping.

I looked up at George, and I just said, "Stretcher – blanket." Then I put my right arm under her shoulders, with her head resting against me, and the left arm under her knees, and so carried her up. I laid her on the stretcher. "You'll be comfortable now my dear." I did exactly the same with the other one. I stood up and waited for some smart Alec to make a snide remark, but nobody did. I cooled down a bit after I had smoked a cigarette. I wonder why I had been so angry.

---

[1] Joan Bartlett and Violet Pengelly. Later, when recalling the incident, Bill said he was in tears when he learned that the girls were called 'Vi and Joan', the same as his daughters.

Joan Bartlett (right) and Violet Pengelly (next to Joan)[11]

I mooched around for a while, then I told the Major about Herb Martin, and said it would take more than one man to get him out, so he sent a couple of men over to do it. I understand the two girls

[1] Photo: Island History Trust Collection

belonged to the Auxiliary Fire Service. Back to the depot 5.00 PM feeling depressed. Some activity tonight, nothing dropped very close, and were not called out.

Have not written much lately; nothing of great moment having occurred, and it is pleasing to note that there have been more bombs than casualties. It's becoming expensive to kill English people.

Me and Vi have still got our U.X.B. over the road, and nobody has bothered about it. Salvaged a few items from the depot. Among them a copper shield that had been mounted on a wooden shield, held for swimming, and the metal scroll from another trophy for athletics, together with some tubes of oil paint which I shall someday use, to try my hand at painting.

Lew Smith, who lives a few doors away, is the agent of our landlord, has been sent from the town hall to lake charge at the depot, and after a chat with him he said, "You haven't paid any rent for some time now Bill, what are you going to do about it?" I said, "I've got one room with a boarded up window, two doors that have to be propped up, the rest of the house uninhabitable, so out of 15/6 for the whole house, what would a fair rent be for the one room?" He could think of nothing suitable to say, except, that I couldn't stay without paying something.

I said I would look for another place to live, and in the meantime, I would act as an unpaid caretaker of our one room. He didn't see it that way, but he reluctantly agreed.

Anyway, he has a book full of empty, or wrecked houses, so he has problems and I have problems, more worrying than he.

I saw Dr. Blasker today, and having nothing else to do, walked with him to his surgery in Manchester Grove, asked him several questions on anatomy, and he straightened me out on them. He invited me in, and he sat me down, got a book from his bookcase, and gave some tutoring, and spent a pleasant half hour. He asked after the two little ones, and the wife, then asked how I was feeling. I told him I was OK, except for a twinge of pain under my left shoulder blade when I took an extra deep breath. He told me to strip to the waist, stuck the end of his listening pipe in his ears, and the cold end all over my chest and back. When he had finished, he asked if I felt fit for work, so I said, "Yes." "I'll give you a certificate to go back to work," he said. I told him I had not been off duty. He flopped back in his chair, folded his arms across his chest and said, "You, my boy, have been running around for three or four weeks with pleurisy, and you are now getting over it." "I wondered why I had toothache round my ribs," I replied. With a big grin on his face, he said, "Get out of my surgery, you're wasting my time." When I got to the bottom of the stairs, he called out. "Ah! Mr. Regan, come in and see me whenever you are passing." He cheered me up no end, and if it were not for the war. I might even feel happy.

Dr. Morris Blasker

To the depot to meet Vi, and have a meal at the canteen. Home 6.00 PM. Sorted out all undamaged household effects. Goldfish bowl broken, fish have died. Will have to leave our beds behind when we have found another place, as they are now ruined. We have salvaged enough crockery, cutlery, and cooking utensils, to see us through. The big dining table is OK, except for scratches and scuff marks, but the two carvers, and four chairs are firewood. All my cycling, and wireless magazines and plans are ruined. Water pipe has burst, and soaked them all. I have found three useable odd socks, a pair of cycle shoes, 1 pair of football boots, 1 pair of very good dancing pumps, 1 pair of scruffy working shoes, two working shirts, a trilby hat, a white silk scarf, and a winter overcoat. A much bigger wardrobe than I expected.

Our poor little cat has been missing for some weeks, and I fear she is dead. Must stop now, I can hear distant gun-fire, and wireless has cut to half power. Alert now sounding. P.S. Have saved my gramophone records, and my S.T. 600 radio-gram.

Poor rest, we woke every time a bit more cement, or a lump of congealed soot rattled down the chimney and onto the hearthrug. A few bombs fell close by, and we could hear some houses come down, with a great clattering of roof tiles; noises I have not noticed before. I suppose there is so much noise usually, we probably treat it as normal background to an incident. Gave up trying to sleep, so got up and lighted two candles, stood them in two saucers, took one out to the scullery, poured the last of the clean water into the kettle, put it on the stove, and Oh Joy! When I lit it, it delivered a full head of gas. We enjoyed that cup of tea. Vi wrote some letters by candlelight, and I waited for eight o'clock.

Depot at 8.00 AM. To Kerby St, to salvage for people who are having to move out.

Saw Ringshaw with three of his men enter a house, after a little while an old lady came out, looking lost, so George Jillings and I, took her along to some ladies who had come from a rest centre, very capable and calm, who took over. We went back to the house, but no furniture or anything else had been brought out. I have a nasty, suspicious mind, particularly where Ringshaw & Co are concerned.

I said to George, "Let's see what is going on." We went in, and listened. They were upstairs, so I quietly said to George, "When you're ready, upstairs quick." We pelted up the stairs, and surprised them. Alf B. and Ernie H. have got some of the drawers out of a chest of drawers, and they both are pawing over quite a big heap of what I think is cheap jewellery and trinkets, but they evidently think it real. Ringshaw is smart, and quick. He says, "Take all the drawers out, it will make it easier to get downstairs." Me and George are blocking the doorway, so having little room to move, we fall for the empty chest. So we carry it down and out to the street, where I saw Lew Smith. He is the man in charge of the depot. I told him should go and see what is going on upstairs. He did. When he came out again, he said, "It's alright, they can handle it. You and George move up the road and see who else you can help." He went away, and we wandered off in search of a coffee-shop.

Back to the depot at mid-day. After dinner, kicked a football around for half an hour, then out to the houses fronting Saunders Ness School to pull down the party walls that are a hazard. Depot 4.30 PM. Played a few games of cards in the boiler house which is still habitable.

Alert at dusk. Raid seems to be widespread; it must be difficult for the guns to concentrate on one target. More searchlights in operation than usual. One bomber came over the depot, very low, flying north to south. It was so low and slow, it must have been in trouble. The mudchute searchlight was the only one able to pick it up. We could see the tracers from the Bofors going into it, and it still kept going. Suddenly the rear-gunner opened up, and after the second long burst, the searchlight went out, and after a while the

Bofors stopped. The bomber was still flying. Went to Lead St[1], but not needed, so came back via West Ferry Rd. Stopped once by a policeman who pointed us toward Gaverick St, but found nothing of consequence. Warden hailed us at the approach to Kingsbridge, but the bomb had fallen inside the dock, near the Keg and Drum, so that was out. Back to the depot, and out immediately to Byng St. The shortest route was straight out the gate and up Alpha Rd, but a huge crater at junction with Mellish St made it impossible, so went to West Ferry Road, turned right and on to Byng St, where we dismounted, and searched in all the Andersons we could reach. The people in all those shelters that were occupied, all O K., and insisted on staying put, so we turned into Alpha Rd. Our lorry was driven at walking pace, up and over wreckage, from Strafford St to Maria St. Alf Crawley, our driver, told me his wheels did not touch the road all the way. When we had finished our searching, we found no casualties and nobody needing assistance, which by the amount of devastation seems more than a miracle, but was quite true, but I worry that we may have missed some although it seems extremely unlikely, we knew what was needed to be done.

Alf had stopped the lorry at Maria St, the men got in the back. I got in the cab with Alf, and as he let in the clutch, there was an almighty explosion from behind, and a rain of bricks, tiles, and anything else that had been elevated, was now coming back to earth. Everyone in back of us got out smartly, but definitely, not with elegance, and tried to scramble under the lorry for protection. The rain only lasted for half a minute, or less, and except for Eddie Sullivan and Bert Forbes, who both had slightly dented helmets no harm had been done, so they mounted up again. Alf looked across at me, and raised his left hand and pulled an imaginary forelock,

---

[1] Short street across Westferry Rd from the lead works; almost next to the fire station.

and said, "Where to, sir?" And of course, I did the proper thing and said, "Home James, and don't spare the horses," and at that, there was another explosion right in front of us, at the junction with Janet St. It was as bad as I expected, we felt no blast, but a big column of earth and clay, back on us, doing no harm at all.

We decided to walk back to the depot, as Alf said it would be impossible to drive through safely in the dark. I got out of the cab, and George Jillings strolled up with his hands in his pockets. He looked in the cab and said, "Hallo Alfie mate, you alright?" And Alf said, "No. I'm just beginning to worry." "You got no worry Alf, they've got it all, upstairs," and he pointed to the sky. By now the other five of our lot had dismounted, and were gawping up at the sky. Alf got down and joined us, and we are looking at the biggest, and most beautiful barrage we had thus far seen. Searchlights from all points of the compass, and shell bursts as far as we could see; there could not have been enough space left for planes to fly. All this going on, and we had not noticed it, being probably wrapped up in our own little world. Alf said, "You lot had better keep your eyes lowered, all that lot has got to come down." We stumbled back the last hundred yards to the depot, and found that Mrs Warren, the cook, had been in with her husband, made an urn of tea and cut sandwiches, and had gone back to her shelter. Very nice, we helped ourselves, but thought it would be dangerous to walk ten yards to the boiler house, in the open air, to tell the other two squads who have been busy all night. They were probably asleep anyway. We ate their sandwiches for them.

We sat and talked among ourselves, until Sid Masefield came over from Major Brown's office, which is now set up in the metalwork-cum-woodwork centre. "Would we like to go back to Alpha Rd, to check an Anderson shelter?" Would we <u>like</u>? We went off in pairs. Eddie Sullivan came with me. We roamed through the back gardens between Cheval St and Alpha Rd, from Janet St onwards. It is still lively, but not concentrated on our little area; we found a few Andersons still occupied, and all the residents uninjured, and seemingly happy. Of course, all the garden walls were now low enough for us to walk over. We get to Malabar St, and the end house, has a higher wall than the others, and there is a chunk of it left, with a door still standing. Eddie says, "Oy, don't tread on the flowers, use the gate." Before he can open the door, we hear a high pitched whistling, rushing noise, and we know it's close. There's an explosion and one hell of a draught, as if someone has left all the doors open. We are both still standing, and Eddie has the door handle in his fist, but the door has gone away. "It blew out of me hand." He sounded offended. We did a bit more scratching around, and then decided we were flogging a dead horse. The All Clear goes, and it's getting light, so we go back. We gather up Jillings. Bracken, and Nobby Clark, and we can see Alf Crawley near our lorry, so we join him. We have a short conference, and to get the lorry back home. It took over an hour to cover about a hundred and fifty yards to the depot. There were a couple of holes, too big to fill in, so got some roof timbers across them, and laid street doors over them, and with the nearside wheels on the pavement, and the offside running on the timbers, proceeded triumphantly to the depot, and got choked off for eating all the sandwiches. Whatever we do, we can't win.

Had breakfast when the ladies arrived, then Vi came along, so as she became busy with the cook. I went home.

I must find some more writing paper.

Document 4. (Loose papers, sheets 1-9)

Christmas and New Year's Eve 1940

We have had a few quiet nights over the Christmas period. We had been alerted, but nothing serious had developed. Those of us who worked through the 'holiday' period, will be taking their leave in the New Year, but I have managed to get three days of my leave, starting tomorrow. Vi and I have pooled our sweet coupons, and have shopped around, wherever we could, and have a nice selection for the two little ones. Bill Bracken and Bert Forbes gave me their rations of chocolate to add to mine. (This chocolate was a token of appreciation for the courage and dedication of our brave, unflinching rescue workers, to be served up on the weekly pay parade.) Hitherto, I have been concerned with getting the casualty out, without causing further injury, and particularly, not shifting anything that seemed likely to bring the whole lot down, and I have an aversion to being squashed. There is one adjectival attribute I must work on. The next time a bomb seems to be heading for me, I shall try not to flinch. Getting back to Billy and Bert's gesture: their reasons for not eating chocolate were weird, and credible if taken with a block of salt. Bert Forbes said he had been told chocolate was fattening, and too much fat was bad for the heart, and wishing to become an old, man, had given up all sweet things. Billy Bracken had a more plausible excuse. He said, too much sweet eating rotted the teeth, and he was taking great care of those he had. This was true, I had seen him take them out after every meal, and give them a good scrub. I did not try to thank them. I just said they were bigger liars than Tom Pepper. Bert said he knew he would become expert at something, and thanked me for pointing it out to him. Billy just said, "Come away Bert, he'll be licking our boots next," I think they like me, but there we are, people have peculiar fancies. With a bit of luck, another three hours and we will be on our way to see the children.

30th-31st December 1940

Whatever may happen in the next few days, must wait, until I get down on paper, the way we got home from Lidstone; and if our Joan and little Vi[1] get to read this, which I very much hope they do, some day in the future, they will know their dear mother much better than a normal life could ever tell them.

When we said goodbye to the children, we were offered a lift in an M.G, sports car, belonging to a young RAF officer who had met my sister in Enstone, and was returning to his base, and would put us off at Southall, which was as near to London as he could get us. We accepted the offer; it would save us a few hours on the train journey, and who could resist the chance of a fast ride in the best little sports car to date?

Went past Oxford at dusk, and at West Wycombe it was really dark, and just before the town we were stopped at a police barrier, where two officers questioned us, and allowed the RAF through, but not we civilians. One of them pointed towards London, and it dawned on me, we had not been seeing the lights of London as I had thought, but the distant glow in the sky of a big fire. In a mere two days of village life, we had lost all memory of the war, and were thinking in terms of returning home from a short holiday. I didn't like the awakening shock.

One police officer suggested that we try to find digs for the night in Wycombe, but I convinced him eventually, that if I didn't make an effort to get back to the depot, I would be regarded as a deserter, which of course was rubbish. He looked at Vi, then said,

---

[1] Usually called Ann.

"What about the lady?" and Vi just said, "I want to go home." The two officers looked at each other for a moment, then one jerked a thumb towards London, and said, "Off you go, and be careful." We went. Our RAF friend dropped us off at Southall Station, wished us luck, and drove away.

I waved our return railway tickets at the barrier, but the collector was busy looking elsewhere. We got a train, as far as it went; I think it was Earls Court. I'm not sure, as twice we had been put off, then on again, but we got to Aldgate, so that was alright. We were going in the right direction.

There were stacks of people on the platform, and stairs. We had heard about people taking shelter in the Underground, and amusing themselves with a sing-song before bedding down for the night, but these weren't singing; perhaps they were having an off night.

When we surfaced, a warden was at the top, sitting on a chair, behind a miniature blast-wall of sandbags, "Hey you, you can't go out there." So I said, "Why not? - we've got tickets." So he says, "Oh, you're a clever Dick are you? You know there's a bloody big raid on." I said.

"Yep, seen one and you've seen the lot, but it's alright mate, we're in the same business." After a little more chat, he said, "Where you going?" Vi piped up, "We're going home," he says, "Where's that?" and when Vi said, "The Isle of Dogs," he rolled his eyes upwards. "You're both barmy, or else you're taking the Micky." I said, "No, straight up mate. Any buses going past here for Poplar?"

He was most impolite, and told us to "P… off, you give me a headache." We went off giggling like two little kids. Gardiner's Corner, a couple of hundred yards away, and still standing, looks lovely, and there is a bus stop just handy, and a bus went past before we got there. I told Vi there would be another one along soon, so we stood in Gardiner's main doorway and had a good look round. We had stopped our silly giggling, and were beginning to realise what was happening, and could see it was a big concentrated raid. All the city seemed to be burning, like the first few raids on the Island, and I'm not enjoying it; it's not background noise any more. I'm just waiting uselessly for a bus. Then Vi said, "What's that awful screaming noise? It sounds like horses." I said, "That must be from the stables behind the Minories, where the brewery dray horses are kept, and don't get any bright ideas, we're waiting for a bus." Then a bus came across from Commercial St, and shot right past me, and another one on his tail. I'm beginning to get angry, so I went back into the doorway, and I told Vi that the next one would stop, or run me down. "If it stops, don't hang about, get on it, if it doesn't stop you'll have to walk home." How daft can you get? After a while, another bus comes ambling over the crossroads, so I jump out in front of it, waving both arms like an irritated traffic copper. The driver stops the bus, and leans on the wheel and says, "Blackwall Tunnel only mate." So I said, "That's far enough for me, old mate." Vi was in a seat near the conductor, and I stood on the platform, fishing in my pocket for the fare money. I said, "Two to the tunnel." He wouldn't listen, said, "Have this one on me." I told him of the other two buses that had ignored me, and he said they had probably forgotten to put the cat out. Funny people, these men, worrying about the cat on a night like this. We carried on talking about nothing in particular, and watching the fireworks, and the bus is creeping along nice and slow so the driver can have an eyeful when Vi pointed out, to a lovely great chandelier of flares with parachutes attached to it, slowly sinking to the ground just behind us. Vi asked the conductor to stop the bus, and he automatically pulled the bell cord. The driver pulled up, and Vi says "Can I get off for a minute?" The conductor says to me, "Here, you're not letting her go and pick that up are you?"

I said, "Not likely, she thinks it look pretty." I have hold of her hand, and she just sits looking at it as it slowly burned out on the road behind. And Vi says to no-one in particular, "Doesn't it look so beautiful? I'd love to have it." By this this time, the conductor has got back to normal and rung the bell for the driver to continue, and says, "Never mind darling. It was too big to hang in the front room". Then we discussed whether to get off at Burdett Rd, and down to the West India Dock by Charlie Brown's. Garford St, past the City Arms and on to the depot, but Vi said Charlie Brown's was not a nice neighbourhood, it had a bad reputation, and it was a dreary walk round that way, so we got off at Cotton St, waved to the driver and conductor, and away we went. We couldn't see too well, but we held hands, and got past the High St, but at the Marshal Keate, I realized it wasn't going to be a simple walk home. I suppose they thought the city was done, and now were dropping them before they got to the centre of London, and we could hear them coming much lower than the barrage balloons are usually moored. Most of the Ack-Ack was overhead now, but seemed to be bursting much higher than the planes were flying. After a few minutes standing in the pub doorway, we moved on, and tried to ignore what was going on. We talked to each other, but I can't remember what we talked about.

We crossed the bridge at Coldharbour, but had not reached Manager's St, when everything around us seemed to be alive with explosions, so we sat down on the pavement, and leaned against the wall. Now I knew why they were coming in so low - the barrage balloons were down, because above the usual noise we could hear fighters, and bursts of machine gun-fire, and the zoom away, and roar in for another burst. I said to Vi, "Shall we go?" We stood, and I brushed the dust of her back, and then I thought, "What the hell are we worrying about a little dust on our backs for?" We just got across Manager's St, when this particular bomber sounded as if it were coming for us, and lighter sound of a night fighter chasing it, a machine gun chattering away, and then a sound of falling bombs, unmistakable, three of them, and it was taking such a long time to happen. The first one exploded somewhere close, hours later the next one, closer, the third one was whistling straight for us, and I was pushing Vi back against the wall, and it was taking a long time, and this thing was still coming at us, and I wondered if it was going to take very long to die, then the whistling stopped, then a terrific thump as it hit the ground, and everything seemed to expand, then contract with deliberation, and stillness seemed to be all around. Then Vi spoke, "Bill, the last one didn't go off." I said, "No, it's probably a dud. I wonder if they get their money back, or a replacement." I never asked Vi what she was thinking while it was happening; I wanted to know, but I thought it would be invading her privacy, and why was I already trying to be flippant? We could hear a racket still going on, but it didn't seem to be of any importance. We had had our moment, nothing was going to bother us again in future. We walked unhurriedly along East Ferry Rd to the George, up to Glengall Rd Bridge, and so the depot.

No calls had come through, everyone was in the boiler house, sitting on their bunks, playing cards or just lounging when we walked in. Consternation! A woman in the men's sleeping quarters. Everyone had met Vi, so I left; nipped across to the office shelter, had a few words with Lew Smith, who said I needn't have bothered in trying to reach the depot, under what he called the prevailing conditions. When I went back to the boiler house, I found Joe Marks had won a couple of blankets, and a bunk for Vi, and George Jillings had gone to cook-house and made tea, and gave us a mug each, and everyone settled down, and waited for daylight. Everyone thinks Vi is wonderful, no one even thinks about me.

Document 2; March 1941

19th March 1941

Nothing of great moment until now.

Plenty happened last night.

We were all bedded down in the boiler-house, waiting for calls, but before anyone else got to us, we had our own problems.

A couple of big ones landed close by, then one through the railings, and under the outside wall of the depot, which shook us up a bit.

Then a call came through. Bullivant's had a direct hit, and the basement was being used as a shelter[1]. Ringshaw took his squad out, and almost immediately, another bomb landed outside the depot, at the corner of Alpha Road, bringing down the first 4 cottages, so some went across to the site, but someone said they were empty, so we busied ourselves with fire bombs that were blazing in the road. We buried them in earth and rubble.

Fred Harrison, my squad leader, was on depot duty answering calls and had sent the rest of my squad to Bullivant's to assist Ringshaw's squad. I went outside again, and met Warden Ernie Lowther limping along from Alpha Road. He looked as if he had been close to a bomb. He had an injured leg, and had been searching for survivors in Alpha Rd when one landed close and knocked him over.

He asked me if we had the three men out of the corner cottages, I said we had been told they were empty.

He said a man and his teenage son, went in the corner house to be with the man who lived there, (a bus driver) to keep each other company. He went with me to inform Harrison, who told me to gather a couple of men and start searching.

My brother Bob had been fire-bomb dousing, so I co-opted him, and we set to work. We had got in about eight feet in a shallow, sloping, rough kind of tunnel, but hit the end of a piano, tipped up

---

[1] Recorded 19-3-1941: II.E. Bullivant's Wharf. Index No. 26. Bullivant's Wharf was located at 38 West Ferry Rd. It was owned by British Ropes Ltd who in 1934 built a new building with reinforced-concrete floors designed to be take the weight of heavy machinery. It was appropriately named the 'Stronghold Works'. The heavy upper floors collapsed into the basement when the bomb struck the corner of the building. More than 40 people were killed in what was the worst bombing incident on the Isle of Dogs.

on end, so took turns working round it. By now I thought we were on a lost cause, so I told Bob to take a blow for ten minutes, then swap with me.

I came out, and Bob went in, while I sat on a heap of rubble.

Harrison came out to me, I told him what was happening, so he said they would get more help. A few moments later, brought along 3 men from Ringshaw's squad.

I thought he was at Bullivant's, so what were they doing here?

I relieved Bob down the hole, where he had just reached the top of a head. I managed to clear his head and neck, when Bob poked his head in, and said there was a doctor outside, so came out to him. It was Doctor Kelly. He had attended at the birth of my second daughter, and knew me quite well. I told him the situation, and that the person was alive, but unconscious. Then I heard soft moaning sounds. I told Dr Kelly, who had a syringe in hand, and he said I should take it, and inject the lot into the man. We had a short argument. I told him I could not find a soft spot, so he said stick it in anywhere, but I couldn't t see any sense in sticking it in a hard skull.

I can hear doc making irritable noises, so I backed out, and gave him the syringe, and told him I was not going to stick a 3 inch needle in a blokes head, and kill him, after the effort we had put in, to get him free.

He wriggled down the hole, and out again in a few seconds, with an empty syringe.

He packed his bag and went away, muttering to himself. Bert Freeman came along a little later, and I gave him the torch.

He reckoned we could chance sawing some of the timber away, so we took turns at it, and enlarged the working space. We could not get his feet free, so we decided to try and pull him out. We got him free, and out on to a stretcher. There were no first aid men, or ambulances about, so Harrison said use our lorry. I pointed to one of Ringshaw's 3 men, and said I can't drive, he can. So Harrison told the one I had pointed out, to act as my driver, so I took him, and the other two.

We got to Glengall Rd Bridge, and had to turn back, it was out of action.

Millwall Docks M-Warehouse next to the Glengall Road Bridge after bombing on 19th March 1941.

We turned into West Ferry Road, round to Manchester Road, and straight on to Poplar Hospital.

The reception area had been cleared of furniture, and the floor was lined with rows of stretchers, with hardly space to walk between them.

We found a space for our casualty, and I informed one of the nurses of the injection he had been given, and got him labelled, and as we were leaving, one of the stretcher cases called out in a weak voice, "Bern, Bernard, it's me, don't you know me." I looked at this face - that was a right mess. I don't know who he was, it was so messed up. So I sat on the floor beside him, and I said, "I thought it was you, but I wasn't sure till you spoke." His next words almost floored me, "Are you O.K. Bern?" he says, "Am I?" So it's a certainty he hasn't seen his face, and he can't be feeling his own problems. So I said I had to go, got more work to do, and he said, "Yes alright, get that cut bandaged, ta-ta then." I don't know who he was even now, but when I got outside, young George Jillings says, "Wipe your moosh Bill, you've got a cut on your eyebrow and it's running down your face." I wiped my face on my sleeve, and there were no cuts on me, so not to worry.

Then I had trouble with our driver. He doesn't want to go back on the Island, so I told him his squad had been sent to Bullivant's, so why had he and his brother, and another man been sitting in an Anderson shelter near where I had been working. He got in, and we drove back round Manchester Rd into West Ferry Rd, and as we neared the Ironmongers Arms[1] we could see a faint light showing through the blackout screens. Someone in the back called out, "What about a drink then?"

I told the driver to stop, then I shouted, "One drink and out." The lorry emptied like magic. They gave us our drink, would take no money. When everyone had nearly finished. I watched my driver with a fresh pint in his hand, so I call out, "Let's get going, now".

At the time of writing, the pub had been renamed The Vulcan[2]. It still is.

I enjoyed seeing that untouched pint on the counter.

---

[1] The Ironmongers' Arms was at 210 Westferry Rd (modern spelling), approximately halfway between the Vulcan and the Magnet & Dewdrop.
[2] In fact, the Vulcan and the Ironmonger's Arms were separate pubs.

The Vulcan[1]

Got to Bullivant's, where I saw Ringshaw, who was coping.

I returned the 3 men he had lost.

Back to the depot, where Harrison told me he was making some recommendations.

The depot has been burned out, and he suggested Bert Freeman, and Alf B— . I said, "Definitely not Alf B— . He should have

---

[1] Photo: Island History Trust Collection

been at Bullivant's, as should have Arthur B— his brother, and Ernie H—."

"They showed up at the depot when Bob and I were trying to get our casualty out. You told them to assist but they disappeared into an empty Anderson and only came out when Bert Freeman, Bob and I had got our casualty out," Harrison said. "Well, he drove through all the bombs to get to the hospital, and you asked to have him as your driver." I said, "Yes, I wanted him as my driver, just to make him sweat, and he deserved to, and if you recommend him. I will spill the beans, and I have two others to back me." I have scuppered my own chances. But I shall be happy if I survive the war. Busy trying to salvage what we could, out of the shell of the school.

Vi arrived at 7.30 AM to help in the canteen. Few minutes later Bert Forbes told me she had gone with Bracken to look at the U.X.B. about 50 yards away in Alpha Rd. I ran out and caught them at the gate. I tore a strip off Bracken, told him to go and sit on the bloody thing, but don't take Vi with him. I was so mad, I felt like kicking her back into the canteen, and we were just stepping inside when it went up. I think the lesson was learned. Home at 9.00 AM.

Nothing to do, so had a walk to the Island Gardens, watching the boats going up to Surrey Docks, or down and out to sea. Found it relaxing[1]. To Allen's coffee stall by Turner's slip-way, where tea and sandwich, met and talked with some fellows I knew, then home at 2 PM to write letters, and catch up on my study of Anatomy and Physiology. Must try to see Dr Blasker to clear up some points. I hear he has moved to Manchester Grove.

---

[1] Within 24 hours of Bill's visit, a bomb killed two people in Island Gardens and one person who was in a boat close by.

4 PM. To the depot to pick Vi up, and I hope, a meal. Took some photographs today. Must be careful, it is 3 years gaol if caught. A Policeman friend of Alf Crawley is to develop and print them. (A policeman?).

Nothing unusual this last week or so. In and out every night, as is now normal. Have had no casualties on our incidents, all the bombs do now is blast most of the ruins.

There are still quite a few people about, mainly men who work on the Island, and sleep in Anderson's at night.

Amazingly, very few casualties among people using Anderson's.

The only one with occupants that have had direct hits was the Elderly's who I have written about. There may have been others, but not on any of the incidents I have gone out to. I have just begun to notice the bad grammar, but why worry? The only people to read these jottings will be my two little daughters, after we have won the war.

Will be going to see them as soon as I can take some leave, hopefully Christmas.

Had a big share of the goodies last night. The Mudshoot has a new man in charge now. They have four big A.A, guns installed, and they used them last night, and what a lovely sound. They go off as one, we can hear the scream as they go up, and follow the sound, and they explode together, forming a square, and if the aim is right, it's got to be curtains for the plane on the end of it.

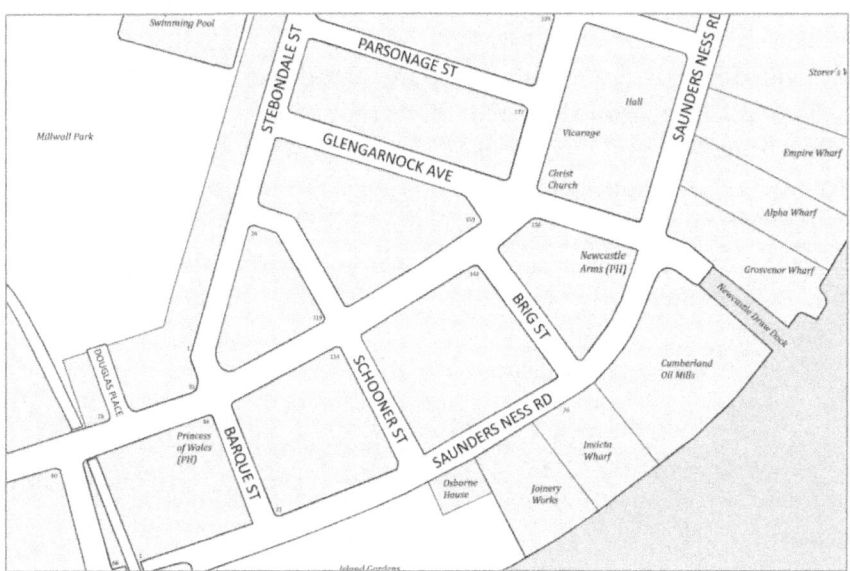

We were out to Parsonage St, found a cluster of U.X.B.s between Parsonage and Billson St, in the back gardens found the wardens and police, moving people out[1]. Back to depot, out again to watch a parachute mine coming down, but it turned out to be a barrage balloon that had broken away. We chased it up Mellish St, grabbed the landing lines, and then wondered what to do with it.

We decided to tie it to a lamp-post, and railings outside some of the empty houses, and along came a couple of soldiers with some of their young ladies, so we left them to deflate it, and went back to the depot, just in time for another call-out to Parsonage St.

---

[1] Recorded 19/20-4-1941. Index No 9. High Explosive Parsonage St and Billson St.

A real mine had floated down and set off the 4 U.X.B.s[1]. It took out all of Parsonage St all of one side of Billson St, the other side was wrecked but not flattened, the Stebondale St end, and the Manchester Rd end, and parts of one side of Newcastle St were totally wrecked, but parts still standing[2]. We found a man clambering about, he said he stayed in his shelter thinking the four U.X.B's would be safe for a while. He didn't appear to be injured, and he wandered off. There were no casualties, as daylight came took photos.

Billson Street

[1] Recorded 19/20-4-1941. Index No 9. High Explosive
[2] Confirmed. Op, cit. Index No.9

HEAVY RESCUE SQUAD WORK ON THE ISLE OF DOGS

Parsonage Street and Billson Street

Parsonage Street from Manchester Road

Newcastle St (later renamed to Glengarnock Avenue)

20th March 1941 (Probably)

Back to the depot 11.30, dinner in the canteen, out again 1.00 o'clock, Millwall Dock, inner, dock police would not let us in, so returned to depot, in time to see mortuary staff cleaning and shrouding 6 bodies.

I could not recognize any of them, but they were Islanders, apparently from Chapel House St.[1]

---

[1] In fact, it was Hesperus Crescent. In Ann's transcription, this incident was estimated to been written in September 1940. However, the only fatalities due to bombing in Hesperus Crescent were registered on 19th March 1941. Four dead were registered, so perhaps the remaining two victims who Bill saw shrouded were from another bombing incident.

Only one of the mortuary staff had any close contact with dead bodies, their senior member, and was the official in the coroner's mortuary for Poplar, but he soon had his men broken in.

The school playground shed had been screened off for the cleaning and shrouding; I never saw them coffined. It was fine, warm weather, and the shed was wide open, with the bodies lying on the asphalt; he soon, by order and example, had his men stripping off what clothing remained on the corpses. "Now wash em off," he says, and the first one to try had a water-bucket and a sponge, and began to gently wash the face of one corpse with the sponge.

The expert soon stopped that; he wasn't going to have a four hour job.

He ordered two of his men to keep the buckets of water coming, and with a long-handled, well wetted mop, gave the first corpse a good wash, back and front, showed his men how to wrap them in shrouds, label them, and stow them ready for final disposal.

Each one took about 3 to 4 minutes, and as he said, "That's how it's done, you'll soon get the hang of it soon enough."

I don't think they ever did.

After this. I only knew of four fatal casualties being brought back to the depot; the victims that my team recovered were always taken away by the stretcher party, or so-called 'First Aid Party'. Where they were taken. I never knew, but not the depot. Anyway, I had other things on my mind.

We were all wandering around in small group, feeling useless, wondering what tomorrow would bring. We soon learned that tomorrow is never, now is what matters.

Manuscript Fragment 5. May 1941 (Estimated)

Nothing of great concern to us happened last night, apart from the usual noise, and a few bombs that caused havoc among the ruins. No. 1 Squad sent to the other end of Poplar. I understand it was Woolmore St.

My lot, No.2, were sent to Hesperus Crescent, that's where leader Ted Wilkinson was killed a few weeks ago, together with another member of his squad, a new man who I never got to know.

We found a policeman, who led us to a nice new bomb crater, which, after investigation, seemed to be almost exactly on top of an already existing one; so after some deep thought, we came to the conclusion that the first bomb had cleared the site, in readiness for the second bomb, which had arrived on target, seriously damaging the first crater.

We went back to the depot, the leader made his report, and we settled down in the boiler house until the All Clear.

Our leader wouldn't tell me what he had put in his report.

Home at 8.15 AM. Vi left at 8.30 for the depot, to help in the canteen.

Received a letter from my mother at Enstone, where she is staying with sister Dorothy and brother Ken. She enclosed two short little notes from our children, Joan and Vi.

We miss them very much, and worry about whether they are being cared for; we both make sure we write cheerful letters to them, and hope my mother is keeping an eye on them.

Went to Bob Allen's tea hut, had a cup of tea and a slice of cake, then took a seat by the river in the Island Gardens, re-read the children's little letters, and made myself thoroughly miserable, and almost wished for nightfall; at least then, your thoughts are concentrated on the job you are doing. This leads me to something else that I have given thought.

Of the eight men I have worked with in my squad, none have been cowards and only Sid Packman shows strain.

Poor Sid is very scared but certainly not a coward, he works as hard as anyone.

Some of the men are very funny, and their remarks, if they were told to someone who had no experience of an air-raid, would not be believed.

During one incident, a second load of bombs was coming down, we are still dealing with the results of the first lot; Nobby Clark has a huge chunk of masonry in his arms, and as he was casting it away, there is an explosion quite near, and Nobby staggers around in a flaming temper, raises a fist to the sky, and shouts, "Come back you German bastards, and I'll screw your bleeding head off."

Or George Jillings, on a close encounter, saying, "Try again mate."

Then, Eddie Sullivan, when the bombers seemed to be on a return run, "You missed, now sod off and let someone else have a go."

Usually, the noise was ignored while you were working.

I feel much better now.

Manuscript Fragment 6.

…we can, but we have the choice of a number of houses, a little better than ours, the drawback is that the people who left them did so for the same reason we are leaving ours.

Jackie Bowers has just been to get some of his belongings from the two top rooms we had sublet to him, and tells me that he and his wife Maudie will be staying with her mother.

I have managed to fill a kettle and one large saucepan with water from the dribbling tap, which should last us for a couple of days, and after a mental debate with myself, I used a pint or so to shave myself and have a cat's lick wash.

I decided to walk round the Island to see what damage has been done.

From our house to the Pier Tavern is looking sick, number 263 is still occupied by Bob Collier. 259 by Ted Chastell, and 257 the estate agents by Lew Smith, so I carried on round the bend to

Seyssel St, where the houses backing on to the Saunders Ness School are looking sick.

The first four or five houses, although they took as much blast as the school, still have their party walls standing, and a couple of them still have pictures hanging on them.

One house has a row of china tea-cups, unbroken, still hanging on their hooks, the rest of the dresser has joined the wreckage below.

The garden wall of the first house is still in place, but the close-boarded fence that topped it, is lying on the pavement.

I remember that fence very well.

During the First World War, about early 1916, Fred Smith who was then about thirteen years old and the leader of our gang of boys, had carved the initials of five of the girls who lived in this row of houses, very neatly on the last panel.

I heaved at the fence until it was free of debris, turned it over, and there was a neat line of letter.

ER. NC. EG. DL. BL.

Edie Rogers, Nellie Cox, Eileen Greenaway, Daisy Lavender and Bessie Lavender.

I wonder where they are now.

This has become a depressing journey, right along Saunders Ness Rd to the end of Island Gardens, hard by the old railway station. And George Allen's tea hut, where tea and cheese sandwiches raised by spirits a little.

I wandered along as far as the Magnet and Dewdrop, but the poor old Island was so wounded I could not carry on, so I went to the depot and cadged a free dinner from Mrs Warren.

HEAVY RESCUE SQUAD WORK ON THE ISLE OF DOGS

Document 5: (Loose papers, sheets 1B-5B)

May 10th 1941[1]

What a night to remember. A lovely moonlight night, and everything was normal for the first half hour after the alert. Plenty of activity, but not particularly concentrated, just shared out amongst us; more of a nuisance than of concern. A few of us had been taking a look around outside, then going back inside for a smoke, while the majority were playing cards, or just chewing the fat. Alf Crawley, who was now No 2's driver, came in to me and said quietly, "Come outside and have a look, and see what you make of it."

I didn't make a meal of it, just glanced up and caught Eddie Sullivan's eye, and shook my head slightly, but he's a wise old bird, and he sat still; but a few minutes later he's behind us.

"Getting warm Alf?" he says, and Alf says, "That's what I thought." I mentally agreed; it was less widespread, and the Mudshoot was firing almost vertically, we could hear the shells going up, not over and away. Most of the noise was above us, and the noise of the aircraft engines sounded like a few more than one.

While we are standing there, in the partial shelter of a collapsed doorway. Sid Masefield came running from the office, and when he saw me smoking, he skidded to a stop, and bawls out, "Put that light out, there's a raid on." Alf said, sarcastically, "I knew all that noise was trying to tell us something." Alf can be a very likeable putter-down of egos. Masefield actually stamped his feet, and says to me, "Put that fag out, or I'll report you." I can't match Alf's

---

[1] The raids in the night of 10th / 11th May are generally accepted to mark the end of the Blitz in London.

sarcasm, so I just said, "Get stuffed." He left us. About two minutes later we heard his lot go off. He had barely cleared the yard, when Harry King came galloping across the yard.

As he went by. Eddie calls out, "Trouble Harry?" Harry shouts out, "Yes...." We can't hear the rest, he's already down in the boiler house raking his mob together. Alf said to me and Eddie, "Come and see the performance." So he led the way to where King's lorry was parked and we waited. Harry would never make corporal in the army, he is too easy going, and his mob is very sloppy. They come spilling out, and Harry is waving them on, and bawling. His driver, Charlie Andrews, has already come from somewhere, and has his motor already started. (I asked him later, where he had come from, and he said he had been in the driver's cabin, watching the fireworks.) One of the mob is trying to run, and get his second boot on at the same time, another one is stumbling along with his gas mask dangling from one hand, and is trying to stuff his axe in his belt with the other hand.

Alf is standing by the driver's cab door, and me and Eddie are standing by ready to slam tailboard up. The last man up was 'one boot', and he looks like he's not going to make it, so Eddie snatches the boot from him and flings it on board, while I am offering my clasped hands as a step. What I don't know is, that Eddie is going to give 'one boot' a boost from behind, so when I take his weight. I straighten up and toss him aboard, but the total amount of shove, is too great, and he finishes up in confusion and a load of loose tackle that should not be laying on the floor. We up the tailboard. I wave to Alf, he bangs on the driver's door, and bawls out, "Get going Charlie." Charlie revs the engine, engages the clutch, and takes off smartly, spilling everyone backwards, but the tailboard held.

When we had stopped our cackling, and soothed our aching ribs. Alf offered the opinion that we were callous to laugh at the incompetent. Little did we know that we were going to be feeling useless before daylight.

HEAVY RESCUE SQUAD WORK ON THE ISLE OF DOGS

We go back inside, and the rest of the men are very quiet, and Eddie has his hands in his pockets, and looks all round, and then he says, "Right, when is the funeral then." And just as he got the words out, there is a huge thud and an explosion, and another of the same, only closer. I said to Alf, "Let's see what's happened," and we clambered up the steps and out into the open, and I swear there is more junk laying around, including a couple of lengths of cast-iron railings that should have been outside in the street, decorating the front of the school. We didn't bother walking through the double gates into the street, we just walked over the eight-foot boundary wall; it was lying flat on the ground, broken into three or four huge chunks.

Across the road, the cottages have diminished in size, they had been plastered before, now they were more so, and we didn't bother investigating. They have been uninhabitable, and unoccupied for a couple of weeks, so we wandered about twenty yards along, and found a big hole, on the same spot as another bomb had struck, a few raids ago.

I said to Alf, "this is the hole that took a day for five of us to fill in." And he said "That's right, now someone has pulled the plug out. Isn't it sickening?"

We can see the N.M.U. warehouse, next to the depot, has flames showing through the gaps in the walls, but we are not greatly concerned, there is nothing much left to burn, and by the look of the sky, ours is only a flicker, so we made our way back to the depot.

Old man Trice, is sitting in the gate-keeper's cubby-hole, with Bill Kerby, but there is not enough room for Alf, Eddy and me, so we move across to the canteen, and stand in the doorway, watching the shell-bursts, and the chandeliers floating down.

Eddie reckons it's a better display than the Crystal Palace ever put up.

There is a balloon coming down, burning, it's not Maconochies, its further away, looks like Deptford. Then Alf says, "Here comes Harrison. I'd better get the motor started," and he departs, while me and Eddie move smartly towards Harrison, when he gets close, he shouts in my ear, "I am duty officer, get them out to Janet St, it's a land-mine," and he's off like a shot, back to the office, over the Handicrafts building. Meanwhile, Eddie has run over to the boiler-house, and bawls out "Number 2, come and get it you lucky lads".

Manuscript Fragment 7. 11th May 1941

Home 8.30 AM to chaos.

Looks as if there's been a fire; the scullery and back room looking decidedly second-hand, everything by the look of things, having had a good soaking.

Ted Chastell and his young son came in. Tells me they heard a near explosion, and knowing Vi usually slept in the front room by herself when I am on duty, had been worried that she might be needing help.

From their Anderson, they saw our house, at the back, is well alight, so they got their stirrup-pump and a bucket, can't get into our scullery for water, so get over the wall to 273, fill the bucket and start pumping.

They are about to give up the struggle, when four firemen come through from the front of the house, and soon had the fire out, squirted water generously over everything, including Ted and his boy.

As he finished telling me all this Vi arrived.

She came over and flung her arms around us. I like the occasional cuddle, but this was not the usual sort, it was too emotional, and no wonder. She had met an acquaintance of ours, who told her I had been killed at an incident.

Whilst she is blurting this out, with her head on my shoulder, she suddenly pushed herself away and said, "Where is our clock?" We had spent months paying off this chiming clock, and now a bloody fireman had swiped it. We thanked Ted and his boy for their efforts, and begun to tidy up.

Vi had spent the night at her brother Tom's place at West Norwood, and had slept well, and about time too.

Bill had started his diary on 7th September, when raids first commenced at midday. The last heavy raid was on 10th May 1941 and these are Vi's recollections:

"More fire-bombs than anything else, and high explosives set fire to the Island everywhere. She had gone to Norwood with her eldest brother, Tom. On returning the next day, she met an acquaintance in the Greenwich foot tunnel who thought Bill had been killed. On arriving home, she found total chaos: a fire bomb had landed on the house, and everything was wet, as fire-buckets were used to put out the fire.

After this, they decided to look for another home but had no luck until a Mrs. Cook, who ran a grocer's shop on the Island, recommended Beckenham in Kent, as there were many houses for rent there. Later they managed to rent a property at 8 Gordon Road, Beckenham, via a friend called Mrs. Kent, who lived on the Island, and advised them of a Housing Agent.

Bill subsequently left the A.R.P., and returned to his trade of bricklaying.

By then, the Blitz was over and the V-1 and V-2 rockets were yet to come..."

Violet ('Vi') Regan with daughters Ann (aka 'Little Vi') and Joan. Photo taken a few months later in the Regan's new home in Beckenham, on the return of the girls from evacuation to Oxfordshire.

PART II
JAN. 1942 TO SEPT. 1944

Saturday 10th January 1942

Vi is taking the kids back to Lidstone[1] today. They didn't want to go, but they made no fuss. I got to Garford St. 8.45, very cold. Went to get my lighter, which is being repaired, not done yet, it's been in his hands 5 weeks. Elmers End 1.15. Talked with Joe Jefferies. His daughter was married today. Home 1.30. Didn't trouble to eat. Went to the Odeon; the only film worth remembering, was the *Commandos on Vaagso*[2]. Home about 8.00 PM. Fried a rasher, 4 sausages, and 3 slices of bread, several cups of tea. Bed about 9.30 PM.

Sunday 11th January 1942

Up about 10.00 AM. Freezing hard. Breakfast, rasher. 3 slices fried bread. 3 cups of tea. No dinner, can't afford it. Made some rock-cakes (they were), cleaned the place up. Smoked and read until 4.00 PM. Made the bed in the children's room, as Vi likes it better than our room. I made a big fire to warm the room. The bed, comprised of 5 blankets, 1 sheet, 2 quilts, and both the children's and our eiderdowns. Vi always complains of being cold, she won't tonight. Vi got home at 9.00 PM nearly frozen. I had hot tea, bread and jam, and the rock-cakes. I told her, how cold it would be in bed tonight, and followed her upstairs to see the effect of my

---

[1] Small village in Oxfordshire. 3 miles from Chipping Norton, where the children were evacuated.
[2] Probably Bill meant *Commandos Strike Vaagso & Maaloy*, a film recording of British Commando attacks on the Norwegian Islands.

preparations. It tickled me to see how pleased she was. I like giving her pleasant little surprises.

Monday 12th January 1942

Awoke at 5.45 AM. Freezing hard, so remained in till 8.00. Made a cup of tea for myself and Vi, and got back to bed to drink it. Vi rose at 9.00, brought my breakfast up to me in bed. Dinner at the British Restaurant 9d, and rotten dinner it was. 1 potato, 1 piece of carrot, and 2" x 3" rectangle of boiled beef, followed by a small piece of boiled pudding, spoilt with evil tasting sauce. It is supposed to be run on a non-profit making basis, it is not. To the Odeon, next door, 9d each, and saw Bing Crosby in *Birth of the Blues*, and *Murder Among Friends*. Both good pictures. Tea at 5.15 PM. Bread and cheese, pickles, bread and jam. Bacon ration for this week finished, just enough cheese for a few sandwiches to take to work tomorrow. Don't know how to pay the rent next week, we already owe one week. 28/-.

I lose 17/- today, and 12/- for this month for H.P, on 3 Piece Suite, is due. A war, no work, and exhortations to 'save, lend, and economise on spending', plastered on walls and windows, or pushed through the letterbox. (Save – what?).

I see that both Russia and China are expressing displeasure at the dilatory handling of the war in the Pacific. China offered to send men to defend Singapore, offer declined. Bed at 9.30 PM.

Tuesday 13th January 1942

Up at 6.00 AM. Frost all gone. At Greenwich and Millwall a little snow, but temperature 4° above freezing point, so I worked. Only the leading hand, one labourer, and I, turned up.

Trying to snow all day. Very miserable. Queued for bus. Millwall; and Greenwich, for a tram. What a rotten service it is, to Catford, always waiting, sometimes as long as 30 minutes (Shut up moaning). Home at 6.05 PM. Lovely dinner. Meal, potatoes, cabbage, swede, Yorkshire. Plenty of it, followed by hot tea. Loafed and read, before big fire all evening, radio dull. Layer of snow outside. Work tomorrow - unlikely. That means no pay. What an existence. Will we <u>ever</u> have State Control? The end of this war must be the beginning of better conditions for the backbone of the country. Enough of this, it makes me want to kick somebody hard. Bed at 11.00 PM.

Wednesday 14th January 1942

Up at 6.30 AM. Thick snow. No work. Signed on at Labour Exchange, given a grey card, to go to Glaucas St; was given a broom to do snow sweeping. Work with a coloured Canadian. Charlie Johnson. He is in the Merchant Navy, now on the sick list. Gassed in the 1914-18 war, and still suffers from it. Canadian authorities could not grant him a pension; said he must go to England to apply for it. He came and got nothing. The Medical board said it (was) too late to open up the case. That was ten years ago. Now, men treated like this, are to be conscripted for this war. We have short memories, or do we realise that we are 'in' too deeply to kick now? Earned 14/5d today. Home at 6.00 PM. Lovely meat pudding, potatoes, cabbage, swede, and hot tea. Some of Sunday's rock-cakes left over. As hard as a moneylenders heart. The RAF could drop them on Berlin with good effect. Bed 10.30 PM.

Thursday 15th January 1942

Up at 7.00 AM. No more snow, but freezing again, decided to wait for the postman, instead of going to work. I had an idea a letter was coming from Poplar Town Hall - it did. Went to Labour Exchange for release form, then to the Town Hall, and was signed on again in my previous capacity as Leading Hand. (Bricklayer £.4/7/0 at 24 hrs.) Rescue officials, and the boys are surprised that anyone should get out of the Service, and volunteer to return. I am told I have put Habberley's nose out of joint, as Freeman entered the navy today, and Habberley wants Freeman's leader's job, but is afraid I will get it. I don't want it. Vi is knocking on the floor for me to come to bed. It's 10.55 PM so bed.

Friday 16th January 1942

Up 6.00 AM. Early on the job for once, when the boss came at 10.0 AM. I beat him to it, by telling him I was finishing tonight, and I found he was going to finish me next week. Bought a jar of Mustard Pickle on the way home, they are very scarce now. They are good, no carrot or turnip to spoil it. The war-time abortion contains about 50% carrot and turnip. Horrible concoction. Walking from the station, the thought came to me that I would find Stan or Dan[1] at home. It was Stan. Comfortable evening round the fire, talking. Bed at 12.30 PM.

Saturday 17th January 1942

Up at 6.30 AM. Decided to go out with Stan at 10.0 AM. Milk ration sufficient for one cup of tea each so Stan and I stopped at Lewisham for tea and sausage sandwich. Bought myself and Stan 20 cigarettes each. Stan to Charlton. I, by 108 to Bromley-by-Bow. Arrived 11.40 AM. Nice surprise - pay-clerk gave me £.2-16-0. Settlement for tools lost in the fire at the depot last March. Rigged out with new uniform at Devon's School. Couldn't find my old helmet. Millwall depot 1.30 AM. Large hot dinner, with Liz the cook. Couple of pints with Alf Crawley at the George. 8.00 PM. Slept in with George Jillings and Harry King. Good sleep.

---

[1] Two of Bill's brothers

The George, on the corner of East Ferry Rd (left) and Glengall Road (right).[1]

Sunday 18th January 1942

Up at 6.30 AM. Home at 10.00 AM. Surprised at the number of the boys, who shook hands with me, and expressed pleasure at seeing me back again. It's nice to feel you are generally well liked. (This will surprise Vi). When I got home today. I slipped £.2, under a loaf, and I was as pleased, with the pleasure she showed, as she was, at the unexpected windfall. That will pay the rent, up to date. Went to Downham, with Stan, to see Ox Miller. To the Tavern, for a few 'wallops', then home to a good dinner. Winkles for tea, a great change. Not had them for about a year. To the

[1] Photo: Island History Trust Collection

Tavern again at 8.00 PM. Too cold for Vi. Home at 11.00 PM. Supper, cheese and pickles. Bed at 12.00 PM.

Monday 19th January 1942

Up at 6.30AM. Took up a cup of tea to Vi and Stan.

He said not to tell Bob, he had stayed with me. He says. Bob is always moaning about being hard up, and is full of troubles. Stan says Bob is Grade 4. Suspected T.B. Dr's Blasker and May were suspicious of my chest. I've been x-rayed at St. Andrews, and previous to that, had ray treatment at Little Missenden. I know, I have a really bad chest, and often have pain under the left shoulder blade, and armpit. I also have night-sweats, they leave me, and Vi, wringing with perspiration. Said good-bye to Stan, who is going on to Wrotham today. Depot 9.15 AM. Greeted very handsomely by Mr Tyler. He enquired after the health of 'Fairy', that's Vi. Bennett tried to get naughty, because I was late. But with a little cunning, and a lot of assumed innocence. I finished on top. While Mr Tyler and I were talking, Habberley barged in without 'by your leave', and proceeded to give me orders. I chided him on his bad manners and he being more uncouth than I, I succeeded in chastening him, and puncturing his balloon of self-importance. He was awarded a B.E.M., he himself doesn't know why. To Devon School with Alf. No overcoat. Back to dinner. Sawed firewood. Read *Innkeeper's Diary*, Quiet evening, snowing again. Bed at 11.00 after beating Alf at Chess once, and being severely thrashed by him, twice.

Tuesday 20th January 1942

Up at 6.00 AM. Tea and toast. Left depot at 9.00 A.M, thick snow. Home at 9.45. Vi out to housework. Lighted fire. Swept snow from garden path and pavement and Horlock's. Chopped up firewood, gave Mrs Horlock half. Loafed around the fire all afternoon and evening. Moved radio to front room. Meat pudding for dinner. Bed at 12.00 PM.

HEAVY RESCUE SQUAD WORK ON THE ISLE OF DOGS

Wednesday 21st January 1942

Up at 6.30 AM. Train from Elmers End to New Cross 1/-, yet a workmans ticket is only 7 1/2d return. Depot 8.45 AM. Row with O'Brien, A-Shift, says I had taken his bed. Words with Smith and Clare. I refuse to carry a bed 300 yards from the Handicrafts every day. In the evening went to the office; listen to a broadcast by Bennett. Radio not equipped with short waves, we could not hear it. Perhaps it was best. I hate to hear people 'trying' to read from the script. Do they try to find the most uneducated working man to represent his class? Bed 10.30.

Thursday 22nd January 1942

Up at 6.15 AM. Home 10.15 AM. Lighted fire. Hot tea for Vi at 12.45 PM. Dinner, to the Odeon. Home 8.00 PM. Listened to radio by firelight. Saw Jim Ruan yesterday haven't heard from the kids yet. Neither Bob nor Dan have replied yet. Bed 11.15 PM.

Friday 23rd January 1942

UP 6.30 AM. Another fall of snow, but much warmer. Began to rain at 9.00 AM. Sawed up firewood, with G. Jillings. Gave W. Crawley tin of green paint, for his tank camouflage. Read in bed until 12.30. Willed myself to wake at 2 ½ hr intervals, to replenish fire. I did, but not again. Broken sleep no good.

No. 2 Squad rescue workers Charlie Storrer and George Huscroft outside their seriously-damaged depot in Millwall Central School

Saturday 24th January 1942

Up at 7.13 AM. Clear sky, snow gone, much warmer. Barbers full, no haircut. Home 10.00 AM. Went with Vi to Poplar. She wanted to see the old place again, although it is almost wholly in ruins. Vi bought new shoes and stockings with my coupons again. Met and talked with Edie Clarke. She's promised to visit us in the near future. Talked with some old neighbours from the Island. All wanting to return. They find their suburban neighbours snobbish, and seem to begrudge them the higher degree of safety from air-raids, that they themselves enjoy. Apparently the 'tone' of the place is of greater importance. (Poor, 'poor people'.) Home at 4.00 PM. Tea, corned beef, mustard pickles. Vi fried steak; listened to Radio. Supper, cheese and bread, tea. Vi had cheese and winkles. Bed 10.35 PM.

Monday 26th January 1942

Up 6.30 AM. Met Arthur French at Catford. He said he and Tom, and Lavinia, went to Derbyshire for Xmas. Heard of a scheme for Rescue men to build shelters, fire-posts, etc. Apparently the tradesmen will be paid 5/- per day, labourers nothing. Further comment later. Bed at 11.00 PM.

Tuesday 27th January 1942

Freezing again. Loafed about all day. Gostling came about 5.00 P.M, to say goodbye. He is leaving Poplar for a better position at …. Anywhere is better than Poplar. Nunn is rumoured to be the successor.

Wednesday 28th January 1942

Up 6.30 AM. Home 10.00 AM. Helped Vi with the housework. Mrs Kent came at 3.30. Had tea, and stayed with us until 9.00 PM. Nice, quiet evening. Bed at 10.00 PM.

Thursday 29th January 1942

Depot, 8.30. Nothing to do. Spoke to George Baker.

F. & T. Thorne[1] are to build new sleeping quarters for us, at the depot. Tells me. I can go to work for them. Think I will. Sawed up wood. Chess with Alf. Bed at 11.00 AM.

Friday 30th January 1942

Haircut. Home 11.30 AM. Lighted fire. Only 2 pieces of work left. Ordered some, a week ago, none here yet. 12.45. Vi home. Got 4 cwt from C.W.S, coalman 1.00. Cost 13/4d. Regal after dinner. When we came out, saw a terrific mauve flash of lightning and a walloping great thunder clap. Home, and bed at 11.00 PM.

Saturday 31st January 1942

Early at depot. Smith not in. Montcalm House[2]. Smith in charge. Sawed up wood for roof of garage. Have almost decided to apply for leader's job. Quiet evening. Bed 11.45 PM.

---

[1] Builders and joiners Frank & Thomas Thorne of Manchester Road. The firm also had a workshop on the site of the former East Ferry Rd Engineering Company, inside the dock fence opposite the George.

[2] This was the first mention of new quarters at Montcalm House for Bill's Rescue Squad. It is not clear if the quarters were in or next to the block of flats.

Montcalm House from the Thames.[1]

Sunday 1st February 1942

Up at 7.30 AM. Made tea and toast. Snowing thickly again, 2 or 3 inches. Greenwich 8.55 AM. Had to wait in the snow, with no overcoat, until 9.25, for a tram. Home at 10.10 AM. Odeon at 5.30 PM. *Freedom Radio*. Supper 9.00 PM. Horoscope says, "Striking benefits likely, if you act promptly." I'll try it. Town Hall tomorrow for leader's job, and will speak to H. Thorne about spare-time work. Bed 10.30.

Monday 2nd February 1942

Up 6.30 AM. Points on tram track frozen, so phoned depot I would be late: arrived 9.25. Snowed again last night. Lazy day. Played chess with Alf. He lost his temper again, not because he lost, but because I'm so dud at the game. Montcalm, played darts. Bed at 10.30.PM.

[1] Photo: Mick Lemmerman

HEAVY RESCUE SQUAD WORK ON THE ISLE OF DOGS

Tuesday 3rd February 1942

Up at 6.30 AM. Snowing again. Home 9.50 AM. Lighted fire, made cup of tea for Vi coming in at 12.30. Odeon 1.45. *Sullivan's Travels* and *Seventh Survivor*. Tea 5.30. Opened two tines of Irish stew, given to me by Bert Parnell in Sept: 1940. Still quite fresh. Slept on settee until 8.00. Made tea for myself, and boiled some milk for Vi, and took it to her in bed. Bed 10.15.

Wednesday 4th February 1942

Up at 7.00 PM. Depot 8.15 AM. Town Hall

10.15 AM. Blyth not there. To stores at 86 Bow Rd for boots. No overcoat. Quiet afternoon and evening. Bed 10.00 PM.

Friday 6th February 1942

Up at 6.30 AM. Loafed about all morning. Pay at 1.00 o-clock. To the Handicrafts with C. Crawley, who asked Sparks if he had got the Leader's money yet. He said, "No" and then said he didn't want the job, wouldn't have it. After moping about, he made up his mind to go home, but it was obvious that he meant to go and beg Nunn for the leader's job.

At Montcalm this evening. Lavers gave Sparks a verbal thrashing. Sparks took it lying down. Bed at 10.30 PM.

Saturday 7th February 1942

Home at 10.00 AM. Chopped firewood, gave Mrs Horlock half. Read all day and evening. Bed at 11.00 AM.

Sunday 8th February 1942

Up at 7.30AM. Walked to Beckenham Hill Station before a bus came along, missed a tram at Lewisham Library. Walked to the Obelisk, and caught the missed tram, it was held up by a sand lorry, broken down across the line. Another hold up at South St. Greenwich, frozen points. Walked to Subway. Depot 9.25 AM. Went with Alf and Storrer to Bow Bridge for petrol. After dinner saw Bigwood of A-Shift, home on leave. Tea 4.30 PM. Montcalm 6.00. Listened to radio until 10.30 PM. Bed.

Monday 9th February 1942

Awake at 7.15 AM. Page was awake, but was too lazy to make tea. Last out at 8.55 AM. Brought electric kettle home, and half a loaf. Lighted fire, put new element in kettle. Odeon 2.00 PM. *Hatter's Castle*, and *Jail House Blues*. Loafed all evening. Bed at 10.15 PM.

Tuesday 10th February 1942

Up at 6.30 A.M, depot 8.45. Sawed firewood. After tea, chess. Found that Bennett's broadcast entailed reading script he had never previously seen. It stated, among other inaccuracies, that he had been a 'marine' for years. He never was. How can anyone, calling himself a man, lend himself, to such a low practice; and that, heard over half the world? The truth about the man, would have made quite as good a recital. Nunn visited Montcalm, saw driver Marks at the depot, gave him a certificate for an 'accident free year', then chewed him up for not being at Montcalm. Bed 11.00 PM.

Wednesday 11th February 1942

Up at 7.30 AM. Home 9.45. Chopped firewood. Regal 2.00 PM. *Honky Tonk* and *Female Correspondent*. Home 4.45, listened to radio, bed 10.15 PM.

Thursday 12th February 1942

Up at 6.30 AM. Depot 8.30. All blankets baked, as 3 men on A-Shift have scabies. The palliasses[1] have never been cleaned for 2 years, and they are shared, the blankets are not. Found collapsible

---

[1] Straw mattresses.

desk, and will take it home for little Vi. Sparks appointed leader. Talked over experiences. Bed 12.30 PM.

Friday 13th February 1942

Up at 6.30 AM. Wrapped up desk, half a loaf, and some margarine, took them home. Arrived there 10.30. Lighted fire: Paid milkman. Paid Muriel, grocer's girl, and invited her in for cup of tea. Vi came home at 12.45, to bacon and fried bread.

Went out at 3.30, to get red cotton, and electric light globe. Brought back 2 flash lamp bulbs, battery, light globe, and forgot the cotton. Sewed stripes on. Bed 11.43 PM.

Saturday 14th February 1942

Up 6.30, depot 8.45. Lazy day. Sawed up wood. A-Shift have arranged a dance to be for the benefit of the parents of Ted Wilkinson, who was killed while on duty, last March 17th: It has taken 11 months to give some help to his parents, who were partly dependent on him. Saw G. Bigwood of A-Shift, on leave from the Army. Bed 12.00 PM.

Sunday 15th February 1942

Home 10.15AM. Brought home, bread, margarine and firewood. Had a row with Vi today. She wants to move to Catford. I don't. Suppose we will though. I wanted the kids to spend the summer here, with us. We will never get a better place than this. To the Odeon. Bed 10.30 PM.

Monday 16th February 1942

Up 6.45 AM. Depot 8.45 AM. We had to change the canvas on the beds. I had the dirty canvas off mine, and had nearly finished putting the clean one on, when Habberley came to tell me the quickest way to do the job. He retired abashed, when I told him he had missed the obvious. I had nearly finished mine, he had not even got his dirty one off. Beat Alf at Chess once. To Montcalm, beat Habberley at darts twice. Bed 11.30 PM.

Tuesday 17th February 1942

Up at 6.45AM. Took home half a loaf. 2 oz. of Marge, and 1/4 lb of tea. Got the motor-cycle parts together. Odeon *Hold that Ghost* and *West Point Widow*. Tea, baked beans. Vi bought new shoes for the kids. Bed 10.15 PM.

Wednesday 18th February 1942

Up 6.45AM. Lazy day. Sawed up firewood. Beat Alf at chess once. Bed 11.00 PM.

Thursday 19th February 1942

Up at 7.00 AM. Got a 4-valve wireless all-wave from Bill Thyson. May change for our AC-DC 4-valver, if Vi likes the all-waver. Afternoon. Regal: *Sgt. York*. Home about 6.00 PM. Listened to radio. Decided to change. Bed at 11.00 PM.

Friday 20th February 1942

Up 7.45 AM. Really late this morning. Greenwich 9.00. Phoned depot. O.K. Installed our radio in 5 Hibbert House. Chess with Alf. Some of the men went to play darts. Marks drove then, and did not report when he returned. Smith phoned Sparks twice, to know if the lorry had returned. Sparks said "No," each time. As a matter of fact, the lorry had been home at the first time of enquiry. When Marks came in. Smith phoned again. Sparks then had to do some 'explaining'. It all nearly finished with a thrashing for Sparks. He wanted to cause trouble for Marks. Bed 11.30 PM.

Saturday 21st February 1942

Up at 6.30 AM.

Went to East India Dock Road to get my lighter, not done yet. Home 12.15. Letter from Vi's mother. Brother Tom, with young Arthur, have gone to live with her. Edie had a row with Tom, and has joined the A.T.S.

Sunday 22nd February 1942

Up at 7.00 AM. Depot before 9.00. Lazy day. Sawed wood. Played chess with Alf, still no progress.

Monday 23rd February 1942

Up at 6.30 AM. Home at 9.05. Brought home lampshade. Regal 1.00 PM. *Chocolate Soldier* and *Gert and Daisy's Week-End*. Home to dinner @ 4.30. Read all evening. Bed 10.00 PM.

Tuesday. 24th February 1942

Up at 6.30 AM. Depot at 9.00. Town Hall inquest on the Marks and Sparks controversy. No overcoat yet. Gave W. Thyson new lead for radio. Played chess in the evening. Habberley, and Storrer, went to Buckingham Palace to receive B.E.M. Habberley back at Montcalm 9.15 PM. Said the ceremony was all 'B—s', and he didn't want the medal, no good to him, etc, etc. The liar. Bed 10.45 PM.

Wednesday 25th February 1942

Up 6.45. Home 9.00. Odeon 1.30 *Lydia*. Brought home 1/4 lb tea. 1/4 lb marge. Read all evening. Bed at 11.00 PM.

Thursday 26th February 1942

Depot early. Nothing to do. What a golden opportunity for some gas drill. Bennett and Tyler don't think so.

Friday 27th February 1942

Up at 6.30 AM.

Home 9.45. Received letter from Bancroft Rd, saying I owe £.44-6-0 cost of the children's evacuation. Letter from Miller's Hospital, they want 10/6 X-ray charge for my left foot, done last August, when I smashed my cycle in a crash with a car. Letter from Income Tax people. What a day.

Saturday 28th February 1942

Up 6.30 AM. Depot 9.00. Went to Bancroft Rd. No satisfaction. Chrisp St. Lazy afternoon. Bed 11.00 PM.

Sunday 1st March 1942

Up 7.00 AM. Home 9.30. Lazy day. Odeon in the evening. Bed 10.30 PM.

Monday 2nd March 1942

Up 6.45. Depot 8.45. The canteen prices are revised. Cheese 2d per oz. Bacon 3d per oz. Sardines 2 ½d each. Coffee 2 1/2d. Toast 1 ½ d per slice. Bread and marge 1d per thin slice. They are supposed to get 40 slices per 8d loaf. Cook told me. I could have as much as a pound of bacon, if I ate it in the canteen, but I must pay 4/- per lb, for it. What the hell is a black market? We had all decided not buy the food at these prices. At least two men backed out to day. C. Crawley and H. King, had toast at P/2d this morning. I suppose the other mugs will follow their example. Resolved not to play chess again. No improvement. Bed 11.00 PM.

Tuesday 3rd March 1942

Up 6.45 AM. Home with firewood. Mrs Horlock some. Cleaned the rock garden, found, about 200 bulbs of various types. Odeon after dinner. Read all evening. Bed 10.30.

Wednesday 4th March 1942

Up 6.45 AM. Loafed about all day. Good dinner today, meat pie. Of course. Liz cooked it. Warren always dishes up cold meat, or goes tank-busting with a tin-opening tool. Alf ate all his dinner, and if he does that, it's good. Tea at coffee shop. Corned beef. Nothing in our canteen, but fish, every night. Bed at 10.30.

Thursday 5th March 1942

Home 10.00 AM. Messed in the garden. Dinner, stew with dumplings. Regal. *Black Sheep of Whitehall*. Letter from landlord, wants me to pay the rent exclusive. I don't want that. Bed 9.45 PM.

Friday 6th March 1942

Up 6.45 AM. Went to Bancroft Rd. Offered to pay 12/- per week, cannot afford more. Tied up firewood. Bought 1/2 lb pork sausages for tea. 1/2 lb fruit cake also. Liz cooked the sausages for me. Read after tea. Bed. 11.00 PM.

Saturday 7th March 1942

Up 6.45 AM. Freezing again, but fine. Took home firewood. Vi and I went shopping. Mrs Horlock gave us a bucket of coal. Read after dinner. Woman called this afternoon to see if Vi would do housework for her. Vi had to refuse. She already does 4 mornings a week now. Read after tea, bed 9.15 AM.

Sunday 8th March 1942

Up at 7.00 AM. Depot 8-45. Cleaned up A-Shift's muck. Went looting, got nothing. Tore up floor blocks for firewood. Alf had a reply from 'Cassandra', Daily Mirror Journalist, re our complaint about our conditions. Slept after dinner, read after tea. Bed 11.00 PM.

Monday 9th March 1942

Up at 6.30. Home 9.30. Reassembled half of the motorcycle. Odeon *China Seas*. Home 6.30, bed 10.30.

Tuesday 10th to Friday 20th March 1942

No record kept. Hinton and Jillings called up.

Saturday 21st March 1942

Up at 7.00 AM. Home 10.00. Worked in garden all day. Wrote letters to Mum and Stan. Bed at 9.30 PM.

Sunday 22nd March 1942

Up 7.30 AM. Walked to Brackley Rd before a bus came. Depot 9.15 AM. Loafed all morning. After dinner made a circuit of the

Island for cigarettes. Millwall, Limehouse, Poplar, Cubitt Town; nothing doing. Montcalm 8.00 PM. Played cards, won 1/3d.

Monday 23rd March 1942

Up at 7.00. Went to depot, filled a bag with coal, and took it home, worked in garden until 12.00. Turned some ground for Mrs Horlock. She gave us a bucket of coal. Had words with Vi, because was late meeting her. Odeon *Belle Starr*. Home 5.00 PM. Tea. Worked in garden. Gave turfs to neighbour, very peculiar people. Nice when they want something, don't recognize you otherwise. Sent Stan 40 fags and 1/-. Bed 10.15 PM.

Tuesday 24th March 1942

Up 6.30. Got out late. Turned back because of hole in the heel of my sock. Depot 9.10 AM. Kicked football about after dinner. Transferred tools to another lorry. Had words with Robinson, nearly led to blows. A. Crawley annoyed at having lost his old lorry, which had caused no trouble, for one that was all trouble. Montcalm 8.00 PM. Robinson brought me a cup of tea in bed. What's come over him?

Wednesday 25th March 1942

Up 6.15. Tea in bed. Robinson quite nice. I won't speak to him. Went to depot 7.30, took some more coal home. Home 8.40. Vi still in bed. Up, and out to her work at 9.00. Dug in garden all morning. Vi, home at 12.00 with a coalman, who let us have 4 cwt of coal. Gave him 6d over and a cup of tea. Regal 1.30. *Dr Jekyll and Mr Hyde*. Home 5.30, worked in garden till dark.

HEAVY RESCUE SQUAD WORK ON THE ISLE OF DOGS

Thursday 26th March 1942

Up 6.45. Depot 8.45. Myself, Herbert, and Robinson, went to Quebec and Montreal Building[1], to deliver coal to the people living there. There has been a grave shortage this winter, and when the coalman has some coal, he supplies the people living downstairs, but is too lazy to carry it upstairs, so that they have been without for weeks at a time. We deliver it to them now. Had a jolly time, but I nearly had trouble with some of the people.

One old lady, crawled from the top floor to ask for some, and I sympathetically carry 1 cwt to her flat, and I'm nearly beat when I get there. Entering, I find a robust fellow, and bigger than I, sprawled on the sofa. Granny can crawl down. I can lug it up, he sits round the fire. Result, a few nasty words from me, but no response from him. Another person, had a cupboard full of coal, and wants more, while neighbours are without. 'If you can't get it in mate, put it on the floor'. I do, all over it. One woman, with three kids, borrows the money from another, for 1/2 cwt. I bung a 1 cwt in, and skip out. I took 3/7 1/2 in tips, from those who could afford it. Those who looked hard-up. I would not accept. I side-stepped.

Back at depot 12-45. Smith asked if we would care to wait for our dinner, until Sir John Masefield came, as he wished to dine with some of the men, as they did. C. Crawley explodes. 'I want mine now, I'm not starving for any '---'! Spring poet', he yelps. We others say 'Yes, of course'. Mrs Warren knows of this, and prepares a good dinner. We don't mind a good dinner, but we object to the men having any old muck, and then, when some

---

[1] Five-storey Victorian tenements in Preston's Rd (along with Toronto, Baffin, Hudson, Ontario, Ottawa and Winnipeg Buildings) built mainly for residents who had been displaced by the construction of the Blackwall Tunnel.

person of importance comes down to see the conditions we eat and sleep under, the place is given a spring clean, and a special meal dished up, and that person goes away with the impression that we complain for nothing. We decided to alter it. I hope we did.

Sir John walked in at about 1.00 o'clock, with his secretary, and some half-dozen men from the Town Hall, and other depots. No doubt, a committee to gag us. The gag failed. Sir John was introduced, and then someone kicked off, with the remark that, "The dinner smelt good, and looked it." I open our score with a beauty, "It is good, but we only have this on special occasions, you should come without warning, and catch us at normal." Arthur Bird puts a spoke in, too. Then Herbert and Robinson, with good digs. Later on I put in one about the sleeping quarters and lack of facilities. Smith glares, but comes back with a softener, "We are having the depot rebuilt, you see we've been like this for 11 months." When I drag him in, with the remark "Isn't that so, Mr Smith?"

Sir John asked lots of questions, and wanted to hear of our experiences. Our efforts weren't thrilling, and personal enough for Nunn, so he calls in a Sergeant. What tales he told. He drove Mr Kennard through the fires and bombs, he drove over a time-bomb. He had a wife and child at home, but he had his duty. He knew it was 'do or die'. All with a mock modesty, but with an abundance of 'I's'. (The dirty tramp). Yes, he could see the time-bomb, but he went on just the same, and it blew up just as he got past it. (The liar). I only hope Sir John remembered all he was told. Lord Dawson of Penn, was also there. They inspected the remains of the Depot afterwards. I believe they were astute enough to reject all but the wheat.

Friday 27th March 1942

Up 6.30 AM. Home at 9.00. Worked in the garden. Wrote to Stan. Bed. 11.00 PM.

HEAVY RESCUE SQUAD WORK ON THE ISLE OF DOGS

Saturday 28th March 1942

Up 6.45 AM. Depot 9.00. Reorganization completed. C. Crawley goes to A-Shift. C. Andrews of A-Shift, takes his place. Sullivan. Storrer. Donnelly. Habberley. Robinson, to Woolmore St.

New men arrive for dinner. A good one, and they will be, for a week, until the men settle down. Then, back to the tin-opener. Posted letter, and 40 Fags, and 1/- to Stan.

Sunday 29th March 1942

Up at 7.00 AM. Home 9.30. Worked in the garden. Read in the evening.

Monday 30th March 1942

Up at 6.45 AM. Train today. Just in time for roll-call. Kicked football about, on Mudshoot this afternoon. Asked to play in match, against A.F.S, on Wednesday, I think I will. Went to 271, got football boots and some of the kids things.

Tuesday 31st March 1942

Up at 6.00 AM. Away early home 8.25. Dug and raked rest of the garden. Planted out a plot for the kids. Regal, saw *You'll Never Get Rich*. Reg: New broadcast. Received letters from Mum. Stan, and Mrs Harris. Bed 10.45 PM.

Wednesday 1st April 1942

Up 6.45 AM. Depot 8.50. Very windy. Football match cancelled. I have taken the job of preparing the supper at Montcalm. Got 5 slices of bacon at 3d each. 2 pieces of fish at 4d each. Wright, driver transferred from Woolmore St, has attached himself to me, worse luck. He brought me a new-laid egg for my tea, which, together with 1 lb of sausages, rasher of bacon, with bread and margarine, and tea, cost us 5d each. Walked round the Island after tea. Saw H. Stanton in Mac's[1]. Flags in the Pier. Bed 10.30 PM.

Thursday 2nd April 1942

Up 7.00 AM. Last away. Home 9.30. In garden. Odeon. *Reg'lar Fellers*, and *Shadow of the Thin Man*. Home 8.00 PM. Tea. Sat round fire till 9.30. Bed. 10.30 PM.

Friday 3rd April 1942

Up 6.45 AM. Depot 8.30. Dull today, collection for E. Heath. Goes in the Navy next Monday. (Good Friday.)

Saturday 4th April 1942

Brought home fish for Vi. Was my dinner for yesterday, but I never eat fish. In the garden all day. Wrote to Mum and the kids.

Sunday 5th April 1942

Up 6.45 AM. Late again, arrived 9.30 AM. Kicked football about. Alf Crawley on leave. Shaved ready for Vi. She arrived at 4.45 PM. We had tea in the canteen kitchen. Went to see Tyler in the Office. Smith goes in the Army on Thursday. Talked with a policeman, he told me of an incident where rescue men on B-Shift, went to Little Stewart St to salvage money from flooded basement. The money was not found, although warden had been able to feel the tin containing the money, but could not get it

Some days later, the water was pumped out, but no money-box was found. The four rescue men were afterwards seen by this policeman, wearing new clothes. He says they also had a week's holiday. The missing money amounted to about £50.

---

[1] The informal name for the Princess of Wales public house, 84 Manchester Rd.

HEAVY RESCUE SQUAD WORK ON THE ISLE OF DOGS

Monday 6th April 1942

Home 9.15 AM. Brought home, sauce, tea and bread. Sowed seeds; cabbage and Brussels sprouts. (Hope they come up.) Odeon. *Blood and Sand*. Letter from Charlie, at Saltash. Bed 12.30.

Tuesday 7th April 1942

Up 6.30. Depot 8.45. Tyler and Darby the office today. Played football match against the A.F.S, this afternoon. We lost 4-0. Made myself obnoxious to some of the team, and enjoyed it. Paid 12/- evacuation money this morning. Saw Smith, came to say goodbye. Bath, and to bed. 11.00 PM.

Wednesday 8th April 1942

Up 6.30. Home 8.30 AM. Vi still in bed. In garden all morning. Regal *Dive Bomber* and *Wavell's 30,000*.

Home 6.15. Planted onion seeds. Trimmed edge of lawn. Tied Loganberries. Bed 10.30 PM.

Thursday 9th April 1942

Up 6.30. Phoned depot, arrived 9.00. Bancroft Rd 12/-. Only fish to be had for tea, every day since Jan. 17th, except Sundays. I had none, nor supper either. Beer at Knightsbridge[1], and darts, with Herbert. Potter. Knight, and Forbes. Later on, Wright. Webber made tea. 10.00 PM. Fathead used all the sugar. Bed 12.00 PM.

Friday 10th April 1942

Home 9.15 AM. Dug in front garden. Vi made jam, and marmalade tarts. Letters from Vi's mum, and the kids; wrote letter to kids. Bed 11.15 PM.

---

[1]Probably Bill meant Kingsbridge (Arms), the closest pub to Montcalm House.

Saturday 11th April 1942

Up 6.45 AM. Depot 8.45. Nothing much all day.

Alf and I, finished collection for Smith. Went to sheds at Cotton St with Alf and Wright, for vegetables. Montcalm 9.00. Sausages for supper. Bed 11.30.

Sunday 12th April 1942

Home 9.10. Egg and bacon for breakfast. Vi cooked a lovely dinner, together with over two dozen tarts. In the garden most of the day.

Monday 13th April 1942

Up 6.45. Depot 8.45. Lecture on First Aid. Afternoon, with Avery and Herbert, set out new boundary wall. Weston on today. Wandered about all evening. Supper, sausages again. Wright brought Jam tart from Woolmore St. It was half eaten, nobody paid him. Bed, to read *I Was a Spy* until 12.00 PM.

Tuesday 14th April 1942

Up 6.30. Home 9.30. Paid 10/-insurance. In garden. Odeon this afternoon *Louisiana Purchase*. Home 4.30. Yesterday, took 2 £1 notes to work, in mistake for one. Woman in coffee shop found it out, when I paid for my breakfast. What luck. Writing this until 12.45 PM.

Wednesday 15th April 1942

Up at 7-45 AM. Depot 10.00. First Aid lecture. Nobody is in love with it. After all the people we have rescued, and the tuition we had before the raids started. I suppose it's done to give someone a job, and to give us something to do. Griffiths. York. Readers, Wimpeys, and other contractors, are doing demolition work that we could have done, during this idle eleven months. No, the contractors must be allowed to take profit from war. What a pretty tangle it all is. Tyler stopped me from First Aid. After dinner. I commenced setting out the boundary wall outside the depot. After a while. Weston, the clerk of Works, had a look at it, decided I was wrong, boned it through, found it was right; that cooled him off, so now I may be left alone to continue the job. Tea at 4.30, fish again, so I have 2 slices of cake. Walked about all evening. Bed 11.00, when King, our leader, came in; he's always last in, and is never there at any time after 5 PM until 10.30 PM at earliest. He'll never get caught.

Thursday 16th April 1942

Up 6.45. Home 9.10. Brought home tea 1/4 lb. 2 oz. marge. Tuesday 2 oz. marge, 2 oz. cheese. Today bacon and egg for breakfast. Out at 10.00, to wait for Vi, at the junction. Bought 10 cigs 6d. Determined to give up smoking, rather than pay the new price, 9d for 10. Regal 12.30. *Smilin' Through*. Tea, mashed potatoes, 7 pork sausages, and another, that Vi left. (Pig!) Supper, toasted cheese and bread. Bed 10.30 PM.

Friday 17th April 1942

Up 6.45 AM. Depot 8.45. Montcalm 9.30. As we entered, the phone rang. Weston wanted me at the depot. First Aid lecture again. Must attend them, bet he wanted the concreting done also; but went to the lecture, dodged out for breakfast ten minutes later. After dinner, fixed datums for concrete and brickwork. Mrs. Macarthy sacked, and Maisey. Married women left, widows sacked. Walked about all evening. Bit of a disturbance at Montcalm about 10.45. Papa found daughter being seduced, thrashed the seducer, only gave daughter a 'talking to'. Why? Caretaker barged in looking boozy, accused us of having blown whistle, because of lights showing in the flats. Phone kept ringing, for no apparent reason, every few minutes, evidently out of order. Bed 11.00. No sleep till about 12.00.

Saturday 18th April 1942

Up 6.30. Bancroft Road, paid 12/-, back to pick up window-sash, to take home for seed-bed. Home 10.30. Stan came last night about 9.40 PM. Had gone out when I got home; bought seeds and fertilizer after dinner. Charlie and Flo, with Lavinia and Johnny, arrived for tea, just-after Stan came in. Tea, corned beef, jam and marmalade tarts, with prunes and cream. Stan out to see Ox Miller. I sowed carrot, beetroot, and lettuce after the company went. Stan not in yet. Bed 10.45 PM.

Sunday 19th April 1942

Up 6.45 AM. Depot 9.00. Raked up all the tubing I could find, to make two garden chairs for the kids, radio stand, coat hangers. Alf lost the sight of his left eye, temporarily, this morning, went home this evening with pain in the head and stomach. Went scrounging for glass after tea. Found brass spray instead. One of our men taken ill Wednesday, died Saturday, Bill Mussen.

Monday 20th April 1942

Up 7.00 AM. Home 9.00, with 2 oz. marge, and wire to make small frames for garden. Stan not been in overnight. Arrived 10.30, shaved, washed, for going to Trottiscliffe. Saw him off at the Bromley South station. Home 1.30. Vi planted lettuces Mrs. Sindenan gave her. Radio news said bomb was thrown at theatre in France, and fell in the stalls of the theatre, was picked up by a woman, and pitched among the orchestra. Why pick on the bank, it couldn't have been as bad as that? Sowed onions. Vi made up a parcel of sweets and chocolate for the kids, and a necklace for little Vi's birthday, which is tomorrow. Bed 11.00 PM.

Tuesday 21st April 1942

Up 6.30. Depot 8.50. Started building wall. Vi came over with Edie at 6.30 PM. Edie is not in the A.T.S., she is lodging at Deptford. Gave Vi a spray to take home, also a box of dominoes. Boys broke into a tea-stall on bridge, which had been closed for a few years. Found tin full of 3d pieces, and cigarettes. I pass it every day, but didn't dream of it. (Mug.) Bed 11.00.

Wednesday 22nd April 1942

Brought home another desk for the kids. Also margarine. ¼ 1b tea, some bread. Regal this evening. *Tarzan's Secret Treasure* and *Tower of Terror*. Home 9.30. Bed 10.30.

Thursday 23rd April 1942

Up 6.30 AM. Depot 8.40. Worked on wall. Avery helping, but he dithers and fiddles too much. Peaston on the far end, but he's not a bricklayer. Quiet evening, bent tubing for garden chairs. Rotten dinner, meat pie, meat being all fat. Bed 11.00 PM. (Nunn came, afternoon).

Friday 24th April 1942

Last away at 8.15 AM. Brought home shove-ha'penny board, ¼ 1b cheese. 2ozs marge. Swept kitchen and dining room. Bought lime-sulphur for spraying apple trees. Sowed more peas. I have compromised by buying one 9d packet of fags instead of two 6d packets.

Saturday 25th April 1942

Worked on wall till 12.00. G, Huscroft left to join Marines today. Took window-sash to pieces. Montcalm. Corned beef, sausage rolls, for supper. Exeter was bombed last night. Many casualties. So-called reprisal for RAF smashing of Lubeck and Rostock.

Sunday 26th April 1942

Home 10.15 AM. Took six panes of glass for cold frame in garden. Made light for cold frame. Bed at 2.30, after dinner, up 8.15 (some nap). Bath was raided last night, also. Heavy casualties.

Monday 27th April 1942

Working on wall. Sent for 3 knots of line. 2/6; sent it back, went to 'pockets' myself. 4 knots 1/8. Spoke with 'E. Anderson' in the subway. Bancroft Road. 12/-. Words with King about paying for food. He says he paid Sat, he did not. He can get his own in future. Heavy gunfire about 10 - 10.30, towards Thames Estuary. Bath raided again last night. Hear they are asking for volunteers to help them. I can feel no sympathy for Bath. They did not rush to help us, in our time of need, neither did they show any feeling. I have spoken with several people, who all express the same opinion.

Tuesday 28th April 1942

Home 9.0 AM. Brought home another window-sash. Put in peasticks. Regal this evening. *Somewhere in Camp* and *Manpower*. Home 10.00 PM. Norwich raided last night. Sounds like Jerry's last fling. Brighton. Worthing. Exeter. Bath, and Norwich, in less than a week. He has done what everyone else has failed to do. Struck at the 'luxury-livers, and arm-chair lounging, pay for safety don't know there's a war' people. Rostock has been 'shaken up', for 4 nights in succession. Let's hope it's well mixed by now. Collection for RAF benevolent fund. Benevolence, bah! It's a state duty.

Wednesday 29th April 1942

Worked on wall till 12.00. Bath after dinner. Gave 'Noisy' a pair of overalls for his boy. Norwich bombed again last night. Why all the fuss about 'ancient monuments', when we know of the aerodromes, and factories around the city? Bomb the workers, as well as factories, then neither can produce. It's a civilians' war, and anyway, we are doing the same to Germany (I hope). Alf Bird leaves tomorrow to start work outside. York was bombed last night.

Thursday 30th April 1942

Home at 9.55. Brought home bottom of desk, to make camp stool for the kids, and handles for hoe and rake. Mowed lawn, sprayed apple trees, mulched them, rose trees also. Sprayed Horlock's apple tree, and returned mower and garden chair. Walk after tea. N.E.E, and E.M. was bombed. 7 places all told, tonight.

Friday 1st May 1942

Letter from Mum. Coming to see us in 2 weeks. Depot 9.15. Avery leaves us Sunday. Worked on wall for a few hours, got fed up; gave it in at 3.30. Bought 1 lb of putty for glass of cold frame. 4d. Roamed around all evening. 2 lamps from Clare, for Montcalm (40 and 100 w.)

Saturday 2nd May 1942

Home 10.30. Brought home 2 large panes of plate glass. Roamed round garden all day. Lent spray to No.4 and lime-sulphur. No raids last night.

Sunday 3rd May 1942

Depot 9.30. Loafed about all day. Vi came about 6.30. To the George, with Alf, and Jack Herbert, with Vi, left her to go home, at the subway. Supposed to play snooker at Woolmore St. Opponent on leave.

Monday 4th May 1942

Home 8.45. In the garden all morning. Met Vi, to Regal *Texas*. Home to tea, steak and tomatoes. Supper, cheese.

Tuesday 5th May 1942

Depot 8.50. Nothing done all morning, but kit inspection by Blyth. He wanted me to play snooker this afternoon. Tyler wanted me to work; I worked. This evening he sent a boy to the canteen for me. Wanted me to go snooker. I said, "No." Later on, said Town Hall wanted me to go to Knapp Rd. I refused; too much messing about. Changed beds with Lavers.

Wednesday 6th May 1942

Letter from Mum. Coming to stay about the 15th. Helped spring-clean house, with Vi.

Thursday 7th May 1942

Nunn was to take roll-call this morning but did not. Another catch. Worked on wall. Webber called up for work today. Paid 5/- for 30 sq ft, of glass, mostly plate.

Friday 8th May 1942

Home about 9.30, with some glass. Pair of shorts, and football shirt, which Brown gave to Clare, given to me by Clare. Odeon. Terrible row with Vi, all over a little thing, the draining board in the kitchen. We had washed the kitchen walls, and Vi tried to fix the draining board, and I lost my temper, because she was making it worse, and would not wait for me to do it. We slept separately, tonight, after I had straightened up the kitchen. I called her many names of which I am ashamed and sorry, but had I not. I am afraid I should have done her an injury, or burst. Whatever happens, I shall never again raise hand, or speak ill to her.

I attempted to strangle her, much to my shame and discredit. But together with the fact that I have very little intercourse, the opportunities I have of going with other women, (which I shall never do) and her coldness making her think that I am too ardent, all mounted together, made me mad. If she knew the frequency of other men's demands on nature, in comparison with my few demands, of sometimes less than twice a month, she would be, perhaps, different.

If she were not born, I should still be unmarried. I would have nobody else. Why don't things run smoothly?

Saturday 9th May 1942

No work this morning. Peaston, Williams, King, Wright, and some others, absent. Did nothing all day. Party held above us tonight; what a row! Police came after Ginger, for showing lights.

Sunday 10th May 1942

This is the anniversary of the heaviest air raid on London, we at Poplar, receiving most attention. Home with more glass. Very quiet between us, all day. Rained this afternoon, the first for some 3 weeks.

Monday 11th May 1942

Arrived early at the depot, causing consternation among the personnel, who are so used to my persistent lateness. Worked on wall till 5.30 PM to oblige Tyler, who wanted to see one panel finished. He has no authority. He tells off the men for certain jobs, if the men don't feel like work, they wait for his back to be turned, then grease off. Some refuse point-blank, and he merely turns away, and works some 'willing horse' to death. He moans about the very little work that A-Shift does. That's as far as he gels. Watched Home Guards at street fighting.

Tuesday 12th May 1942

Home 8.25, with more glass, and 3 pieces of fish for Vi. Odeon after dinner *Keep 'Em Flying*, and *Man at Large*. Shove ha'penny after tea.

Wednesday 13th May 1942

Early at depot. Raining, no work. Tyler wanted me to work under a sheet after dinner, but I told him I wouldn't do it even when I was working for my living. Tea at 6.00 o'clock, when Vi phoned to say Mum, Dorrie, and Ken, had arrived to stay a few days. It's the first time Vi has used the phone, her voice sounded nice. I got my pass, and got home at 7.40, where I found also Mrs. Kent and her daughter Ida, with her child Jean, a nice little child, who took to me at once, as all kids do. Stayed till 9.20. Back at depot 10.40 PM. Cancelled my leave until next week 22nd. Uniform not cleaned yet. Leggings issued. Took blanket home. Nunn came this afternoon. Mum asked me to try and get Ken apprenticed to bricklaying. I think the office staff, such as Surveyor's Dept., or Estimating Clerk, would be better. Brought home 2 pairs of football stockings.

Thursday 14th May 1942

Home 9.00. Vi did not go to Mrs. Lindenan today. After dinner. Mum and Ken went to Bob at Becontree. Dorrie would not go.

Friday 15th May 1942

Early at depot. Getting too regular. Worked on wall. Peaston is no bricklayer. Reverses the bond, gets straight joints in the work, and gets above the line. Cut up half of our old table-tennis top, to make the kids a doll's house. Wright was in today, after 3 shifts absence. He has fixed up cricket match for Tuesday, and I am to bowl. Let's give 'em some Larwood! Alf and I bowled a little, after tea. Bennett sawed off some hand-rail, and took it home.

Saturday 16th May 1942

Up early. (Made draining board Sat. 16th). Started for home but had to turn back. I had left my respirator and helmet out. Home 9.20. Mum and Ken not back yet. Vi and Dorrie, still in bed, so took than up a cup of tea. Mum and Ken back at dinner time, with a crab and kippers. Slug and ant killing after dinner. Ants got into larder, and were exploring crab, which Mum washed and had for tea. Mum told me of the way she was robbed by her brothers and sisters, of money bequeathed by her father and aunt. Some few thousands, a little of her father's life: Wilson family, of Hanwell, Middx. Owners of sawpits; of Uncle Bill Wilson stealing her father's diaries, and family records which she says were wrapped in red turkey twill, and labelled 'to my daughter. Miss L.E. Wilson'. After tea, Vi and Mum took Dorrie to Eltham where she will stay the night with her young man's people. Back at ten, and with Ken and I, to the 'George IV' for a drink.

Sunday 17th May 1942

Phoned after Catford. Depot at 10.00 where Tyler was waiting, wanted to know if I was going to work on the wall. I didn't know whether he was serious, and said so, but he was. I told him, my religious obligations debarred me. He is getting to be a 'tartar'. He declares that when the depot is walled in, he will give everyone plenty of work and keep them at it all day. Waited for Ken, at the Subway till 2.15. To Poplar, bus to Paddington. Mum, Ken, Vi, Dorrie and Fred, her young man, just arrived 2 minutes after me. Fred to Charing X. Vi with me to Millwall. Saw Jim Rose at Eastern. Tea, and bowling practice with Alf for 1/2 an hour. Another pair of football stockings.

Monday 18th May 1942

Telegram from Mum. She had left ration books etc. Posted them off. Dug plot for tomatoes. Transplanted cabbages.

Tuesday 19th May 1942

Depot at 9.00 AM. Weston on today. He and Bennett tried to stop Wright and I from going to cricket this afternoon, but failed. Weston said he would have us working till 5.00 PM. The Town Hall stopped that. No work on wall (no sand). Played Shoreditch, and lost by 3 runs. (41-44 all out). I had one swipe, caught out for 0. Got 3 wickets on one over, two clean bowled, one caught. I caught one off Storrer. Capt. Evans. L.C.C. Clerk of Works, came to the office; wanted to know if I would undertake brickwork on damaged schools. I was having dinner when he called, but I finished it before going over to the office; he had gone when I got over there. Am to see him Thursday. Weston told him the rate was 2/3d per hour, it's not, it's 2/0 d. But I told him to leave it at 2/3d. Clare goes in the Mary next week. C. Crawley is back at work on A-Shift. I have spoken to Bennett about some gas drill.

Wednesday 20th May 1942

Home at 8.35, with plywood. Bought liquid manure, and sulphate of ammonia, for vegetables. Regal saw *Johnny Eager* and *Two Latins from Manhattan*. On the way back we enticed a pretty tabby-cat to follow us home, it did.

Thursday 21st May 1942

Worked on wall until 12.00, rained after dinner. Vi went to Poplar Town Hall to get a job as a warden. She was told there that they don't want any, and are going to sack 200 of those they now have.

Friday 22nd May 1942

To Bancroft Rd, paid 24/-. Home 11.10 AM, to bed with headache, the first I ever remember. All the men in depot, with a few exceptions, were up through the night, with diarrhoea and pains in the stomach. Rotten grub again. Letter from Mum. Vi wrote to her mum. We both wrote to the kids.

Saturday 23rd May 1942

Worked on wall till 12.30. Tyler got King, our leader, to work on spur-stone at side of gate. Tyler can't get the men to do anything he wants. They simply ignore him, so he turns on any mouse-like dispositioned person he can find, and shouts and bullies at him, thinking he is being authoritative, and he always picks on King. Instead of getting the gang to do it, does it himself. After dinner. Herbert and I, finished the capping on two piers. Hearing Tyler tell Ginsberry, and some others, to go and clear the pavement of bricks. Herbert and I went to see what would happen. Forbes and King came along, and we told them, so they hid when Tyler came along, and he got to work on shaping the cement spur-stone himself.

After a while, Forbes, and King, came out of hiding, and watched him do it. Herbert and I went through the baths next door, and approached from the strut. The men told off to clear the pavement, did not, so after trying to rope me in, and failing, he, (Tyler), did it himself. After tea, Vi came over, so she, Herbert, A. Crawley, Forbes and I, went to the George, and after leaving Vi go home, we others, minus Crawley, went into the London; Carden arrived later, and we finished with a sing-song. Back at depot 11.00 PM.

Sunday 24th May 1942

Home 10.00, and to bed after breakfast, until dinner at 2.00 PM. Bed after dinner. Played shove-ha'penny after tea!

Whit-Monday 25th May 1942

Depot 9.20 AM. Being a holiday, no work, but Herbert and I feel good, he helped me to build a pier, to pass the time. Vi arrived at 6.30 PM. Went to the George with Crawley, were joined later by Herbert, who had taken his wife and child to Greenwich Park on the afternoon, and played what he called silly asses, also Potter. Circular tour to the London, Pier, Princess of Wales, where Alf and I left to see Vi on to a tram at Greenwich. Back to Herbert and

Potter, then to the Lord Nelson, where Crawley would drink no more. To depot, and played pontoon. I winning 4d. Bed 12.00 PM.

Tuesday 26th May 1942

Home 9.30. To bed. Up at 1.00 for dinner. Bed again till 4.00. Vi to the Odeon at 5.00. I prepared tea for her return at 8.30. Shove-ha-penny, and to bed.

Wednesday 27th May 1942

Worked on wall. Tyler doing the labourer's job, getting bricks for me, while the men played cards. Got a cricket ball, and with A. Crawley had some bowling.

Thursday 28th May 1942

Home 8.30. Met Vi. 12.30 at Memorial, dinner out; to the Regal.

Friday 29th May 1942

Tyler not in: Bond: worked hour or so. Meeting to start sports club. I am elected Chairman. Refused to be sports representative. Wright accepted. He is more 'in' with the Town Hall. Bowling practice this evening.

Saturday 30th May 1942

Stayed behind to discuss matters with C. Crawley secretary for A-Shift. Attended their meeting; home about 11.30. Stan Bensley and wife (was Ada Kent), and child came to tea. Stan and I went out for a few drinks, to Three Tuns and George and Dragon. Nice evening.

Sunday 31st May 1942

Brilliant weather today. Early at depot. Meeting held in sports room. Everything smooth. Bowling for half an hour before dinner. After dinner laid down to sleep. Alf woke me at 2.00 for more bowling practice; I didn't want to get up, but he would not let me rest, so I practised. After tea, everyone went to Woolmore St, for a concert. Alf and I remained behind. Watched Alf beat Tyler at chess several games.

Monday 1st June 1942

To work for Harry King. General house repairs. It will enable us to get the clothes the kids are in need of. Home 5.15 PM. Dinner; manured lettuce, cabbage, beetroot, carrot, and Brussels. Transplanted Brussels. Vi uprooted all the bulbs to store. Bed about 12.15.

Tuesday 2nd June 1942

Went to Lead Street with King. Herbert, Wright and Potter, to remove loose slates from bombed houses. Came back in the afternoon, and told the others we had 2/6 each, given to us by the owners. We had not, but the others wanted to have a go at it. Previously it had been too dirty for them. Had a bath. Cricket practice after tea. Bed 12.00 PM. Woke at 2.30 AM. Alert sounded. Heard gunfire. All clear in 30 mins.

Wednesday 3rd June 1942

With Jack Herbert, erected scaffold, demolished chimney slack, cleaned bricks. Home at 5.30 or so. Meat pudding for dinner. Transplanted Brussels sprouts, weeded onions.

Thursday 4th June 1942

Worked on wall, did very little. Wright has done nothing about the sports club. I collected all subscriptions. He would not take charge of billiard table, which was installed yesterday. He said he wanted to go out but he didn't. He went card-playing. Persuaded all but two to join club. Took 1/8d off table. Gave Herbert lupines, some other flowers, and 1 rose.

Friday 5th June 1942

Built chimney-stack. Dinner with J. Herbert. Bought bottle of cider. 1/4 quart. Back to depot to get the particulars about administrative side of club. Half-pint with him. Brown. Crawley.

Stennett[1] and I drank the cider. Home 9.00 PM. Read in garden. Now to write letters to insurance people, and billiard-table makers.

Saturday 6th June 1942

Town Hall, interview with Blyth. Haircut. Posted letters and P.O,'s to Jelks and Insurance Co. Nobody will take a turn at the billiard table, must do it myself. Played snooker. Gave red rose to Doris[2]. Wedding in flat below. Forbes well oiled. Undressed himself in the office to show Tyler his scars. Tyler got worried, thought Forbes was going to get into bed with him. About 2 AM, the wedding party had a fight. When it finished. Forbes blackout shutter fell in, he replaced it, got back into bed, bed then collapsed. Oh! Happy night.

Sunday 7th June 1942

Waited to see W. Crawley and H. Stennett of A-Shift. Home 10.30. Slept all afternoon. Vi went to Mrs. Kent for tea. I would not go. Thinned off beef and carrots.

Monday 8th June 1942

Worked on wall. Gave Doris 2 roses. Bancroft Rd, paid £1.4.0. Nothing else of interest.

Tuesday 9th June 1942

Spey St, with Herbert; plastering. Home 7.00 PM. Sat in garden.

Wednesday 10th June 1942

Admiral Evans giving a speech to 'C.D.' personnel. I was not down to go. Bennett asked me to work on wall; Tyler said I was to stay behind. I told Bennett to go and -----. Told him I would rather go

---

[1] Name spelled 'Slennett' in Ann's transcription.
[2] Child living with parents at flats opposite.

home in my underwear, and give up my uniform, rather than be messed about. Went to Town Hall heard Evans speak; and a very poor dropped aitch speech by the Mayor of Poplar. Dennis, Town Clerk, spoke next, about how good and brave we were, but the strength of the Service must be cut still further, yet we are told to be in readiness for more severe raids. Older men are being drafted in, and have to waste valuable time and money, teaching them. We who know the job, are to be drafted into industry, and to waste more time learning a new job. Played billiards and snooker. Gave Doris 3 roses. Lent Paddy Keane 6/-.

Thursday 11th June 1942

Spey St, again. Home about 6.00 PM. Watered the garden. Vi has changed the bedroom round, it looks much better. Bed about 10.15 PM.

Sunday 14th June 1942

Organised Snooker tournament. Promised that a (mythical) person from Beckenham would give prizes to everyone getting through the first round. I was congratulated for getting in touch with a sympathetic generous person. 32 men entered tournament. That means I have to find 16 prizes. Only Alf Crawley knows I am giving the prizes.

Monday 15th June 1942

Wanstead, to reset tiled fireplace, for a supposed 'gorgon'. Did the job in 2 hrs. Got 8 hours pay for it.

Tuesday 16th June 1942

Worked on wall. First Aid lecture again, but Tyler won't let me attend, he is only interested in getting the wall up. Why don't we have some gas drill? We have had none for nearly 2 years. Too little and too late again, as usual.

Wednesday 17th June 1942

Spey St, with Jack Herbert, distempering. To Mills Drive, and Byron St, nothing doing, people out.

HEAVY RESCUE SQUAD WORK ON THE ISLE OF DOGS

Thursday 18th June 1942

Got a message, saying union delegate was down yesterday. Told to stop work on wall. Dispute about hours and money, so I stood by. Bennett would not ask me why I wasn't working, but kept out of my way, after stopping today's cricket because I was not working. He told Weston I never trouble to work when he (Weston) is on. Weston asked me why I was not working, on hearing my reason, he quite agreed, and said I was in order. Bennett is trying to do me harm for some reason, or other.

Friday 19th June 1942

Left Spey St., went to Portree St. Repaired ceiling and lavatory seat and cistern. King came to say he was in trouble, drain job in Grundy St. Jack and I went there this afternoon, but could do nothing. Home about 6.30. Quiet evening.

Saturday 20th June 1942

Worked on wall. Bennett pounced on me this morning. Gave me a rather garbled account of a visit he paid to Town Hall. Said I was in the wrong, and should have ignored union delegates order. I said it was his pigeon, not mine, and he would have to pluck it. Tyler asked, should he speak about it at the Town Hall. I said he could, as far as I was concerned. What happened? I don't know. Final of Snooker Tournament this afternoon. Fifteen prizes awarded. Cost me 32/-. A letter from the 'anonymous' donor, concocted by me, and written by Vi, was read out by Alf Crawley, and was met with general approval. I am considering a weekly review letter for the club. I'll write one, and see how it goes.

Sunday 21st June 1942

Stayed to see W. Crawley. Home about 11.30 AM. Cleared box room out, ready for Ken to take as bedroom. Same to back downstairs room. Vi got jealous about the roses I have given to Doris. She must have read this diary. It gave me a great laugh. She doesn't know who Doris is. Sometimes she thinks she is a sweet young lady; at other times she guesses it's a child. I won't tell her which. Asked me not to take any more roses until Mum has seen them. I said, "Yes."

Monday 22nd June 1942

Worked on wall all day. Jack Herbert complained of pain in chest. Went to doctors about 5.30 PM. Given a letter to take to London Hospital; got home and collapsed and died on his doorstep. Another good man gone. The best fellow that ever I knew. Left a wife and girl of about 6 years, and son about 16 years. Yesterday Chandler told Nunn I would not work on wall because Peaston had no ticket. (Lying fool).

Tuesday 23rd June 1942

Did not feel like work. Home 10.30 AM. Mum had arrived. Spent all day getting the furniture and beds in order. I believe they will be comfortable here. Ken and Dorrie have to find jobs. Vi was sorry to hear about Jack Herbert. He was to go on holiday next week. (Couple of beers with Forbes and Kay in the Pin[1]. After hearing of Jack's death, another couple with Alf at the George).

Wednesday 24th June 1942

Depot. Loaded lorry. Bennett said, "Exercises 2.30 PM."

Call came 1.47. All caught flat footed. Exercises rotten. Had to remove my respirator. Could not breathe. Nobody knew anything of First Aid. Bennett bounced us in the office afterwards. But later admitted it was his fault. I have had no First Aid instruction. Tyler says the wall is most important. What a mess up! No gas drill for 2

---

[1] The Pin was a shortening of 'Pin and Cotter', the informal and more commonly-used name for the Union public house. Its postal address was 102 West Ferry Rd, but it was some yards up a narrow road which was an extension of Mellish St and which was originally named Union Rd.

years nearly, and efficiency is expected. Nobody seems to care. I have asked for gas drill. It's useless.

Thursday 25th June 1942

Grundy Street. Repaired lavatory, new float. Four ales with King. Forbes, and Kay. Knocked off about 5.45 PM. Home 7.20 PM. Nice large dinner. Quiet evening. Ken starts work in chemists next Monday. Dorrie not working yet. Lent Forbes 10/-. Lent Wright 5/- last evening. I'm getting affluent now that I'm administering the club's finances.

Friday 26th June 1942

Depot 8.30. Worked on wall. Hear Chandler and Macefield have to go to Labour Exchange Monday: 29 to go to work. Gave King 6/2 for last week's Sports Club.

Saturday 27th June 1942

Squared accounts with W. Crawley. Home 11.30. Mum and Ken go to Becontree. Dorrie and Vi to Regal's Dance. Bought shoes 6/-; rubber. Hoed garden. My first weekly review letter was very well received, and favourably remarked upon (Sigh of relief.)

Sunday 28th June 1942

Early at Depot, for a change. Ran a billiards tournament today. Nothing of interest today. Town Hall could give no satisfaction regarding a lorry for Jack Herbert's funeral. Don't know who is going, or what arrangements have been made.

Monday 29th June 1942

Spey Street, to fix new wash basin, sink. Did not see the funeral. Home about 6.00 PM. Vi and Dorrie have been swimming. Ken started work in chemist's shop.

Tuesday 30th June 1942

Worked on wall. Tyler asked me to run a course of 9" brickwork on new concrete. There is 92 bricks in a course. I did it under half-an-hour, between 11.30 and 12.00 midday. He then wanted me to just set the piers out, and finish them off, so with him chasing around, and imposing on a 'willing worker', I blew up, and told him what I really think of him. His skin must be armour-plated. He is more interested in getting a wall round the depot to shut the men in, than getting the depot fit for habitation. He has previously declared to me, his intention of making life a misery for the men, when he gets them back in the yard. Cricket this afternoon at Hackney Arena, against City of London. We lost by 33 to 56. I had the luck to hit out 50th run, and a couple more. None of us could bowl for toffee. Derbyshire invited Risby and I to Woolmore Street for tea. Our canteen never has anything but fish. Thunderstorm this evening. Lend Paddy Keane 5/-.

Wednesday July 1st June 1942

Bazely Street, plastering ceiling. I'm no good at it. Home about 6.30.

Thursday 2nd June 1942

Early again. Mustn't give Bennett any chances to 'fix' me. He's trying hard, since he made a fool of himself over last week's exercises, and threatened to stick to the letter of the rule, and only give half-hour passes, to which I said, it would only affect his friends who went home to tea, and took 3 to 4 hours off to do so. Worked on wall, no cement this afternoon, so went to Bancroft Road, to pay 36/-. Nearly everyone left their dinner today. Meat pie again, making 3 times in 6 shifts. This time it was not tinned meat, it was well-frozen meat, most of which went black. Warren was going to resign, but apparently, it was not accepted. Wright won billiards tournament. 5/-. Slade second 2/6.

Friday 3rd June 1942

Bazely Street again; got a lift to Catford this evening.

Saturday 4th June 1942

Stayed home today. Tried to sweep kitchen flue. N.G. Regal this evening, *Foreman went to France*. Mum went to Downham, to see Mrs. Russell.

Sunday 3rd June 1942

Went for ride on Dorrie's cycle before dinner. Picked and ate our own peas today.

3rd Febuary Lidstone
             Enstone.
             Oxon
             19 4 3

Dear mum dad and all
I hope you are alrite. Our
cold is better and we have
started school to-day.
And we have some nice
sums and I had them
all right to-day. One of
the soldiers fell down in
the mud dirted his clean
trousers and he had just
changed them. One of
the soldiers are just like
uncle Tom. They said
they was going to put
the serchlight on to
night. We we went to
Gypsy Friday with
auntry and bought some
cof cough - sweets from
Well lots of love from
x x x x x x

Letter from Little Vi (Ann)

HEAVY RESCUE SQUAD WORK ON THE ISLE OF DOGS

> The Shewsbury Arms
> Lidstone nr
> Enstone
> Oxon.
> 24 2 43
>
> Dear mum and dad,
> I hope you are getting on all right. Thank-you very much for your letter. I had nineteen marks out of twenty for Dictation to-day. We have got Friday, Saturday, Sunday Mondays and Tuesday off. Gran and Aunty beat the Soldiers at dominos because they havent gone yet. The book said they are staying for eight more months weeks. We are going to have a May-day in May. The Sergent is in here now and a soldier named Paddy. Violet has not been to school to-day because she has had the ear-ache. When our fence fell down did it brake our Rose trees down? For Dinner at school we had, potatoes, Meat-pie and for afters, Chocolate rice. I hope you and dad are better, and I have got another certificate last week, so I have got three now. I have no more to say so good-by for now lots and lots of love
> Joan
>
> ALL xxxxxxxxxxxxxxxx   TIM xxxx

Letter from Joan

Ann's Notes:

"Autumn 1941 to 3rd September 1943

In the summer of 1942, Bill was called for a medical at Little Messenden, Bucks. He was convalesced for 2 weeks. He then returned to the A. R. P., and was sent for a further medical to Poplar Town Hall. He was found unfit for duty but was told he could return if he recovered sufficiently from chest infections and pleurisy. Consequently he obtained odd jobs of repair from the Labour Exchange, and was eventually sent to Doncaster to work on ammunition and bomb dumps at Ranskill. He was lodging with 3 other men, at Mr, and Mrs. Embley's, who became good friends. By January 1942 the contract had ended and he returned to Beckenham.

1943 - The move to Bellingham

Bill and Vi had had Bill's Mum and sister Dorrie to stay temporarily. My Sister and I were also back from evacuation in Oxfordshire. The landlady, Mrs. Davies, then wished to increase the rent from 25/- to double that amount. The case went to court, where Mrs. Davies' solicitor described her husband as an air commando and war hero, so the magistrates were naturally sympathetic. Bill and Vi had no money for a solicitor, and had to put their own case, with no knowledge of courts or lawyers. They lost the case, and were ordered to pay costs. By now, our neighbours were all sympathetic and anxious to help. On the day the bailiffs were due to call, (I remember it was sunny and very warm), we received a letter from L.C.C. (London County Council) offering a place at 27 Overdown Road. Bellingham (this was the road where Henry and George Cooper, of boxing fame, also lived, and I went to the same school as them).

When the bailiffs arrived. Mum showed them the L.C.C, letter, and one of them said, "This is the best thing I could have heard. This is the worst job we've been called to do."

What a time we have had this last few months. Mum has gone to a flat at Downham. We have had notice to quit, and been taken to court over it. The landlady won, we paid 15/- costs. Dorrie and Vi both working at the Admiralty. Vi in the small vessels' pool. Mrs. Davis came to see us several times, told us she was selling the house, but we would not have to get out. Just before Xmas wrote to tell us we must pay 32/6 per week rent, or go. Early in the New Year[1], another letter demanding 30/- or get out. Later on several letters from Mrs. Harris at Lidstone, telling us we were doing so well, we had better have the children home, telegram from Ilkeston to say Vi's mum had died. We had previously been up there to see her, as she was expecting to pass away any time. Vi to the funeral, I to get the kiddies. Ground and water rates demanded of us, that landlord had not paid.

Moved to 27 Overdown Road. Bellingham. Catford, S.E.6.

September 6th 1943

Had some night raids, but the kids sleep through them. Mrs. Harris wrote three times asking us to send the kids back to her. Wrote to Doncaster. Mrs. Embley replied. Wants me to send Vi and the Kids to her. Vi doesn't want to go, nor let the kids go. After much persuasion, we let the kids choose. They go to Enstone[2], Easter, the Embleys stayed for a week. I out sick, pleurisy. 4 weeks before they came, 1 week while they were here. Blasker sent me to St. John's Hospital for X-ray and sputum test. Negative. Only two more weeks sick leave to come.

[1] January 1943
[2] To Mrs Harris, Oxfordshire

Thursday 18th November 1943

Ravely Street this morning. (Something being made out of this job.) The men, the fools, are asking if they have to work here on Sundays. (Ask and ye shall receive, ye mugs.) Took Light Rescue this afternoon, to Strattondale Street, instead of King. He appeared upset about it. Sick money not yet arrived. Nunn and Roberts came this evening, to give Pryor and King certificates from school. Pryor was brought back from Pin. King could not be found. They waited an hour or so for him, left without seeing him. Martin and Tyler roused him when he got back at somewhere around 10.15 PM. To the Pin with Forbes and Bracken. King will fall soon.

Friday 19th November 1943

Bromley High Street. 4" Meter Box for Gas-men. Dirty bricks - no material for scaffold. Wood went home after dinner. I 'waited' on myself. Oh! Misery. Drew Wood's money for him. Gate fell of its hinge while Sid was trying to shut them. Oh! Joy.

Saturday 20th November 1943

Ravely Street. Row with King, before Roberts and Jolly. He told Bracken and I to unload cement. I told him to pick on some of the tough guys who have boasted of their abilities in that direction. Accused him of laying for me, for some weeks, because I can get the men to work for me, they ignore him. I think he holds it against me for teaching the Light Rescue, in his stead. He wanted to smooth things over afterwards. I would have none of it. Exercises this afternoon.

To Maconochies.

Montcalm this evening. Wright and I to Knightsbridge[1] - did not hear Alert, until 15 minutes later we heard gunfire, and got back. King arrived 25 minutes after Alert, trouser-front unbuttoned, collar askew etc. Had been caught in bed with a woman when siren went. Back to her after All Clear. Then back to bed at Montcalm 11.25 PM. Bill Bracken ignored the phone.

Sunday 21st November 1943

Home 10.00 AM.

Monday 22nd November 1943

Up 8.00 AM, took time off, as was promised me. Lighted fire, washed up, and generally useful. To the library then depot at 2.45 PM. Martin out of temper, said I had taken a liberty by taking 5 hours out. Well, he promised it but I'll do him no more favours. Gave up 5 coupons. He says I still owe 4. Cannot have my cleaned uniform until they are paid in.

Tuesday 23rd November 1943

High Street. Leave meter-box, start manhole. Slashed away, but could not finish it. Surveyor, Clerk of Works, and one of the governors present. Home 6.00 PM.

Wednesday 24th November 1943

Ravely Street.

Thursday 25th November 1943

Bromley High Street. This job gets worse and worse. No gear for our use.

Miserable day. (Home 6.0 PM. Quiet evening. Joan better.)

---

[1] Probably Bill meant Kingsbridge (Arms), the closest pub to Montcalm House.

Finished manhole, but no cover yet. Started slabbing in lavatories. Nothing definite about this job. "Size of openings?" "Oh, near enough 3ft - or 2'10", something like that" "Got the Frames?" "No, but you can manage without". Can I, I wonder? What a firm.

Friday 26th November 1943

Borrowed laying-on trowel, from Fred Collier, for rendering wall of sleeping quarters. Back to depot 10.30. Gillingham had started. I caught him up. Trowelled my work. He floated his. Mine better. I think. To the library - shut. Shaved after tea. To the Kingsbridge, 1 glass, back. Warning went. King arrive 3/4 hour after. No incidents. He will get caught some day. Baked potatoes, bread, cheese, onion baked, for supper. Bedding back to depot. Repaid the borrowed 10/- to Bill Bracken. Saw Rockman this afternoon, says I owe 1 coupon. Jacket cleaned and ready, new trousers to come. (Perhaps). Was paid 10/3 back sick pay. Stopped me 10/3 as I should have been in, in the evening (What rot!).

Saturday 27th November 1943

No work today. Straight home. Did the shopping. No eggs again. Slept all afternoon until 6.00 PM. Read during evening. No alert.

Sunday 28th November 1943

Dug-out[1] sweating. Lighted fire in brazier. Winkle thought I was in there, burning to death, so he galloped in to put fire out. Gave Bert Bracken a quarter pound of tea.

Sunday 28th November 1943

Up early. Martin picked a mixed squad to work at Ravely St. Ginsburg. Balls. Hawkins. Wright. Lewington, under King. They all said, "No Work." But they did, and in the afternoon. (They are

[1] Shelter

to get time off later on.) Why can't our officers be straightforward? They could have saved unnecessary friction by telling the men of the privilege first, instead of waiting for insubordination to appear. To the Pin with Forbes. Bed 21.00 hrs. Alert 2.05 AM. All clear 2.15 AM. (Bought 20 Razor Blades 2/-).

Monday 29th November 1943

Up 6.40 AM. Bert Forbes knocked off bicycle at Glengall Bridge, by motorcyclist who did not stop. Bert was three parts of the way over, and the bridge will only take one lane of traffic, but the other fellow couldn't wait. He went in the dock entrance.

Glengall Rd. Bridge[1]

Bromley High Street 8.30 AM. Unhappy day, nothing went right. £2 to Bancroft Road, letters to Avery[2] and Doncaster. Home 6.00 PM. Helped kids with homework. Played with little Vi. (4/- from Mack for sweepstake).

[1] Photo: Island History Trust Collection
[2] Colleague – worked with Bill part-time labouring.

Tuesday 30th November 1943

Worked on wall of sleeping quarters. Rendering. Tyler still making himself a nuisance. Asked did I and Gilliam go to have a drink at eleven o-clock? When Bracken had already told him we had gone for fags. Why not ask outright, "Where did you go?" Very childish behaviour for a man. Still he seems to be getting senile. To the library, got *Mein Kampf* and *Tom Sawyer Abroad*. I see somebody has swapped beds with me. I'll get it back. To the Pin with Bert Forbes - 2 pints. Got a pint of milk for the kids today. Put it into a beer bottle. Half a small heart for the cats. Was my dinner. Borrowed 5/- Bill Bracken.

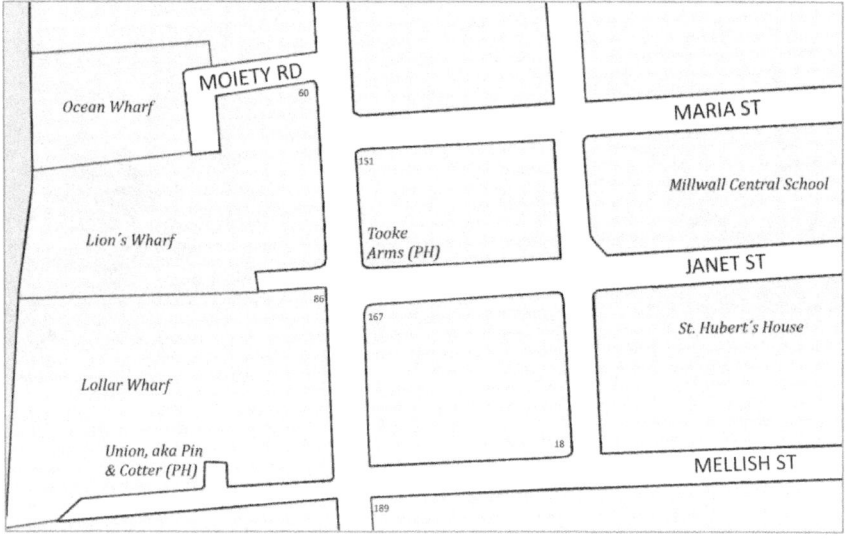

Wednesday 1st December 1943

Up 6.30 AM. To Bromley High St. This job gets worse. No door-frames, or timber, to use for profiles for breeze-slabbing. Erected scaffold, someone swiped it while Wood and I were at dinner. Bought 3 lamp bulbs and pinched one. Gave one to Wood. Home at 6.05 PM. After tea. Vi on settee enjoying herself, making big Tim swear, and tying his whiskers in a knot. Heavy gunfire, heard planes. Dropped twelve flares, some red others white. No doubt trying our Pathfinders' method, but nothing seemed to come of it. Helped Joan with her homework, but she leaves it until she is tired. (Heard yesterday. Wilson gives Martin eggs, what a game! He has been crawling a lot lately. Wanted me to refuse the rendering; he fiddled to do it himself.)

Thursday 2nd December 1943

Raining all morning. Rendering this afternoon. Pay clerk showed me a communication from County Hall, about my glasses. They want a grant from my Society, toward the cost of them[1]. As I bought them myself, asking for a grant from the Society hardly seems fair. I think it is the responsibility of the L.C.C. To the Pin for a couple of Burtons. Slept with Forbes in the gatekeeper's place, as Charlie Tuting was out sick. (Phil did not turn up).

Friday 3rd December 1943

Bromley High Street. Row with the so-called navvy ganger cum bricklayer. Wanted my labourer, Fred Wood, to leave me to cut some holes out for the fitter. I wouldn't have it. In the afternoon, the boss told me a tale of the Clerk-of-Works saying 'not much had been done by me.' I told him to let me speak when the C-O-W comes again. (I don't believe him.) Episode of the 'Harking-Stick'. Drew £1.14.0 Home at 6.05. Queenie. Charlie's Lady-friend, took the two kids to Lewisham Hippodrome. Vi and I to the King Alfred, for a couple of drinks.

Saturday 4th December 1943

Rendering. Phil was leaving at 12.00, when Tyler slopped him, and said he had orders that everyone was to work this afternoon. Phil would have none of it. Tyler told me I would have to work, I

---

[1] Sick Society – paid part of sick benefit.

said, "No." They at the Town Hall are trying to take liberties with us. I asked for an interview with Nunn. He didn't seem inclined to grant it. So I said I would go anyway, and see Nunn. Men from Ravely Street, said the Saturday and Sunday work were all voluntary, and that volunteers would be given privilege leave, according to the time worked. I tackled Tyler about this, he said he knew nothing of this. So I told him to find out. Finally arranged that Bracken and I were to carry on with the rendering, but our names would go down as volunteers, and would be granted the same privileges as Ravely Street men. Ravely Street men back at 3.15. I carried on until 4.15. Won 2/3 at cards. To the Pin with Forbes. Bed in my old shelter 12.00 midnight. Bought 1 dozen Razor Blades - 3/-. No more of that.

Sunday 5th December 1943

Up at 7.15 AM. Took a quart of milk. 1/2 pint shrimps. 1 pint winkles home. Queenie to Dinner. I took little Vi to see Mum at Downham. Northover with Stan (on 48 hrs, leave.) Dinner with Mum, who gave Vi some trinkets and photos, belonging, to Jessie[1]. Home with Stan and Vi, to another dinner. Charlie arrived before 5.00, had a bath and tea, left about 8.15. Stan left at 6.00 PM. Mum has promised to come over for Xmas. First time she has ever spent it with us. Previously been all Bob. Stan says he doesn't want to go to Bob's.

Monday 20th December 1943

Depot 8.00 AM. Rendering.

---

[1] One of Bill's sisters, who died of T.B, aged 19, before the war started.

Tuesday 21st December 1943

Bromley High Street, finished pay-box. Bit of circular work beneath tea urn[1]. To Bancroft Road 12.00. Paid 10/-, found they had received previous 10/-. Home with sheet of plywood. Soaked with rain, had to change all clothes. Queenie came about 7.00. Air raid same time. Lovely barrage lasted about 30 minutes.

Wednesday 22nd December 1943

Depot 8.00 AM. Worked on rendering. Paid out club money, after dinner. Gave King money for sick members. Were paid wages today. Went by tram today in best clothes, uniform still wet. To the Pin with Forbes, Wood, Bracken. Andrews called us back after a few minutes. Nunn wished to speak to the men. When we got back, nothing of the sort. Pontoon. I won about 2/-.

Thursday 23rd December 1943

Bromley High Street[2]. Nothing to do. Wood and I sacked. Got blackboard for little Vi Tried to cut 2 panels out of door, found it was plate glass. Sid promised me another job. Home by 108 bus and 38 tram. Walked from Catford. Home at 5.30.

Friday 24th December 1943

To depot 8.00 AM. Afternoon off for everyone. To Goodrich for plain white cups. 6"- and a glass rubbing board[3] for Vi. 6/6.

---

[1] When Depot was bombed it burnt the field kitchen and brick pedestal built for tea-urn

[2] Bromley-by-Bow. B. did casual work for a firm there.

[3] For washing.

Goodrich's General store at 167 Westferry Rd[1]

Cut up asbestos sheet, to make table mats. To the Pin at 8.30 with Forbes, Bracken, Wood. A fight developed. Found it was Pryor and another. Left them to it. Found Pryor lying on ground outside at 10.30. Forbes and I carried him back. Page had left him. Martin well-oiled. Paid Docker 10/-, he gave me 6 razor-blades. Lewington took the hat round, gave me 5/10 halfpenny. 1 shared with King. Another 6d, later.

Saturday 25th December 1943

Up at 6.45 AM. A-Shift began arriving before 8.0 AM. Another mix-up. Blundell told them 8.00 o'clock. Marlin Tyler said 9.00.

[1] Photo: Island History Trust Collection

Home at 9.50. Queenie at home Breakfast, constipated egg, and bacon. Charlie arrived 12.00 midday. Electric cooker went wrong. Wright and C. fiddled with it. For no reason whatever it started to function again (Hooray). Charlie and I 1 pint at King Alfred. Good dinner at 2.00 PM. Tea 6.00 PM. Played cards and shove ha'penny. Charlie fire-watching at 7.00 PM.

Borrowed bike. Won part of pontoon sweepstake with Liverpool. Joan slept on settee. Tied 10/- note to Christmas tree for Joan. She 2 bicycle lamps. Little Vi big board and easel. I had 100 cigs.

Sunday 26th December 1943

Depot 9.00 AM. Fixed electric fire in shelter. To the Pin at 12.45, with Wood and Bracken. Balls, Forbes and King arrived later. Slept until 5.00. Tyler paid for tea. Martin did not attend. To the Pride at 8.15 PM. Five beers then to the Pole A good fill up, and sing-song until 10.30 PM. Martin well-oiled. Gave away sandwiches, and sausage rolls, and blathered a lot. Walking across the yard in the dark I fell down sink-hole. Found shelter, and fell into bed. Find I have half-share in sweepstake, about 34/6. Paid Moss and Stone and Davenport 10/- each, club money.

Monday 27th December 1943

Up at 6.45 AM. Home at 8.30. Vi. Charlie and I to the Fellowship Inn. Burton and Whiskey. Vi had 3 whiskies. Back to dinner. 1.30, Queenie cooked it. Rabbit pie, beef. York. Potatoes, cabbage, parsnip. Xmas pudding. Slept till 5.30. Played cards with Charlie, little Vi, and Joan. We had to let Vi and Joan have their money back. Charlie and Queenie away at 8.30 PM.

Tuesday 28th December 1943

To Bromley High Street, on Ravely Street lorry to pick up tools. Blundell poked his big nose in again. Back at Depot 10.00. Our gang waited at Ravely Street till 10.00 AM, nobody else turned up. King phoned depot, and Martin sent them to Maria Street. Afternoon no work, for anyone. Took alarm clock back to cafe. Markie paid for it. To the library. Skittles after tea. I won two games. No beer. Received sweepstake money 34/6 - to the club 4/0.

Wednesday 29th December 1943

Up 6.45 AM. Home at 8.30 AM. No-one up. Started to make doll's bed. Mum came after dinner. Gave her £1 for Dorrie, and posted 10/- to R.D[1].

Thursday 30th December 1943

Depot 8.0 AM. Work on rendering. Skittles after tea, alert 30 minutes at 7.45 PM. More skittles. I won 2 games. To the Pin with Forbes, back at 10.30 PM. Billiards with Forbes.

This morning. Tyler went into canteen and roused King, said, "Half a ton of cement on wall, half of that on the ground, go out and look after your men." King wore it. Said nothing of it to me, or Bracken. Andrews told us.

Friday 31st December 1943

Home at 9.30 AM. with 2 batteries. 1 for Vi. 1 for Joan's bike lamp. Took little Vi to the Monument, St. Paul's, Trafalgar Square and Westminster Abbey. Home about 5.15 PM. Marking out new club books.

Saturday 1st January 1944

Early today. 8.00 AM. Tyler not in today. Cement-work wall. Found some firewood. Ravely Street apparently finished. The 'rest' went to Maria Street. Lavers and Hawkins came in today. More Skittles. I won 1. 10.05 PM. Martin gave Hawkins a bullyragging when he came in behind me. Said, "I've a bloody good mind to run you and Lavers, you too Forbes, you're taking f...ing liberties." Hawkins nearly cried, the great fool. F...d and swore filthily at

---

[1] Evacuation money.

Barden also. Said, "I have got to stop here all the evening, while you can go beer drinking - there's no-one to give me a break." Inability to do as the men did was certainly the reason for his disgraceful behaviour. Said nothing to me. These so-called rough guys! They let him bully them unmercifully, and unjustifiably.

Would I? Not if they merit any disciplinary action, O.K. But the filthy language? No. Gave 4/- to Andrews for repairing my cycle shoes.

Sunday 2nd January 1944

Home 9.30 AM. Cleaned bicycle, until 10.30 PM. Joan to the 'pictures' this afternoon. Vi to Sunday School. Played cards this evening, gave Joan her money back. Mum gave Vi her losings back. Vi woke me at 11.55 PM. Heavy gunfire. I got up and went outside. Saw several red and yellow flares hanging in the sky. Shell-bursts to the south really heavy, the sky one continual sparkle, a plane heard climbing, a thick red flash, then quiet. I believe 'they' got it. Watched searchlight for about 10 minutes signalling dot dot dash dot dot. Went back to bed 12.30 AM. All clear soon after.

Monday 3rd January 1944

Depot at 8.10 AM. Bracken and Forbes to go to school at Christian Street at once. No previous notice. Wilson, skilled man, took Bracken's place, labouring for me. Worked till 11.30 AM. No more cement. Nunn came at 12.00 midday. Toured the depot. Tyler turned my electric fire out in the dug-out. He's dead scared. Wash and shave this afternoon. Skittles and Snooker this evening. Bed 10.45 PM. Nunn came again this evening.

Tuesday 4th January 1944

Home 9.15 AM. Bought account book and cards for club. Chimney-sweep came. Vi took the kids to see pantomime – 'Cinderella' at Lewisham Hippodrome. I wrote part of speech for the next club meeting and made a jug of cocoa for the others when they came in. Bed at 10.45 PM.

BILL REGAN'S DIARY FROM THE SECOND WORLD WAR

Wednesday 5th January 1944

Up at 2.20 AM. Heavy gunfire some bombs, and A.A. shell. Cup of tea, to bed again at 3.00 AM. Depot at 8.5 AM. Martin called Roll, first time for 5 or 6 weeks. Gang to Maria Street. Balls and I said nothing about there being no cement, helped Tuting clean the Canteen, when Tyler came in we were cleaning the window. He said, "Good lad, a good idea." King and A. Crawley painting. After dinner, instead of a rest, owing to the early morning Alert, the men had to clean the tools, and clean more windows. The mugs put up with it. The leaders get privileges of going out when, and as often as they like, and in consequence don't trouble about the rights of their men. King seeing Mrs. West home, and Barden on the beer. Played snooker and Billiards, with Forbes and Tuting. Gave Balls 4/- for having my fountain pen repaired, and new nib. Wrote out and dated all club cards. Bed at 11.15 PM.

Thursday 6th January 1944

No Alert last night. Up at 7.05 AM. Home at 8.55 AM. Looked woodworking tools over. Plane wants truing, 2 chisels sharpening. Shall take them to depot tomorrow. Meat pudding for dinner. Chopped firewood. Lay down after dinner until 5.00 PM. Tea. Joan came in howling this evening. I went out after the boy responsible. I think the other girls are using Joan as a whipping-boy. I'll stop that. Later on, other boys outside swearing, brought Joan in.

Helped her and Vi with their homework. Mended a toy Wonderscope.

Friday 7th January 1944

Depot at 8.05 AM. Balls went to Town Hall with correspondence. Martin told King, the leader to mix the compo up for me. Martin seems to want to belittle everybody. I told King I would knock it up myself. We did it between us. Even so, there were labourers still in the depot who could, and should have done it.

Rusby waiting hand and foot on Martin, is one example. There is supposed to be only Tyler and Martin in the office and when anyone from the Town Hall comes, he immediately runs out. To the Pin with Forbes back at Depot at 10.35 having been out since 9.55 PM. Found Martin using the same kind of filthy talk to Barden who had been out too long, but after 10.30 PM. Martin said no matter how long he'd been out, he wanted him in by 10.30 PM. Said nothing to Forbes and I, apparently because we had not been gone more than 3/4 of an hour. (Sharpened 2 chisels and a plane iron today.)

Saturday 8th January 1944

Home 9.00 AM. Carried on with making doll's bed, broke one piece so packed up. Letter from Board of Trade saying I owe 2 coupons for clothing. I don't. Am not going in until 6.00 PM tomorrow evening. Privilege for working Saturday afternoon and Sunday. Took Joan out on her bike to Sidcup, St. Mark's Cray, looked round the Church, and St. Paul's Cray. Wrote letter to Stan. Doncaster, and 10/- to Bancroft Road.

Sunday 9th January 1944

Was going to have breakfast in bed, but got up when I found Vi had dropped her bacon in the ash-tray. I wouldn't have any breakfast. Loafed about all day. Depot at 6.5 PM. Club meeting 6.30. Made out club savings cards collected subs (2 weeks). Played snooker and billiards, 3 1's won 1. Bed 11.20 PM. Understand from Tyler that I must shift from dug-out to sleeping quarters, dug-out wanted for First-Aid stand-by parties. That also means no shelter for the men, should it get really hot. And the sleeping quarters stink.

Monday 10th January 1944

Was going to Town Hall about the coupons and Martin and Blundell. I thought they had left me alone, but it seems they haven't. I told Martin about the coupons 4 times but he would not attempt to confirm it, until Rockman did it about a month ago. It was raining so I went home. Bought some screws on the way home. This afternoon bought another 2 account books. Bath at 4.00 PM. Got Vi to copy out rules of club, this evening. Kid along street pushed little Vi in the mouth, made it bleed. I went to his father about it. One boy 15- I could have smashed his face in, and would, if I had seen him.

Tuesday 11th January 1944

Up early. Depot 8.05 AM. Freezing, so no work for me or Balls, the others went to Maria Street. Asked Martin about taking my blouse to be repaired. He said leave it until Rockman comes. I agreed, whereupon he immediately decides that I ought to lake it. I was to get some tape for Mac, also 7 lb cleaning rags. Martin told me to go to Town Hall about my coupons. That was just what I wanted. When the 'rest' knew I was going, they wanted to know if I intended to speak about the shelters. I said yes, for myself, for them too, if they wanted me to represent them, and would support me.

Saw Jolly and Overton about coupons. Find that none have been credited to me for 1943. Jolly said Briggs at fault. Jolly not cleared on the book either. Roberts came in, so I told him about the shelters. Jolly and he, said they knew nothing about it, except that Nunn wanted the bunk fittings replaced. Said there was no conceivable objection to me sleeping in the shelter. Told him of Blundell's game of bed-snatching. Said the Andersons were for the men.

When I got back, and told Martin and Tyler, Martin appeared very flustered and apprehensive. George Balls came in and afterwards said he thought Martin was going to have a fit. Got a spring bed in shelter for myself. Wonder if Blundell will shift that, it will not fit in the sleeping-quarters.

Skittles after tea. Opened savings club. Pryor 5/-. Andrews 10/-. Winnie 10/-. Wood 2/-. Hawkins 5/-. A good start. Wilson (Mortuary) showed me a pair of prismatics worth 12 guineas, easily, selling them to Davenport. Played James snooker, beat him. Carlile and Livington back.

Wednesday 12th January 1944

Home 9.0 A.M, with some wood. Chopped firewood. Loafed about all day. Did Joan's homework for her. She can do it but is not interested.

Thursday 13th January 1944

Early again. Did some more to wall. King labouring for me again. Went ostensibly to get water for me. Instead went straight to canteen, put a penny on table, helped himself to a cup of tea. Back 13 minutes later. Wright told me. Lavers sick again. Skittles and billiards this evening. Library at 4.0 PM. Got Dover Road again. Alert at 7.20 One gun fired from Mudshoot, that's all. To the Pin with Forbes and Carlile. Carlile and Lewington told me of a tandem cycle for sale. I think I will have it.

Friday 14th January 1944

Up 7.0 AM. Fine day. Paid Bushby 8/10 half penny for Table, and tips etc. Wright 1/9. Home 9.30. Mended chair. Vi got ratty, so I put tools away, and loafed all day. Vi to the pictures with Iris Wright. The kids to dancing club. Wireless off at 8.00 PM. No warning. Vi home at 8.20 PM. Did Joan's homework. Cleaned cycle brake.

Saturday 15th January 1944

Depot 8.13 AM. Dense fog. Only 4 men arrived before me. Worked on rendering with Bracken. Martin put the men scrubbing the canteen out. Being a damp day, they suggested it be done on a more suitable occasion. When Martin was told of this, he said, "If they don't do it. I'll run 'em all." No thought as to the right or wrong of the men's request. But then - they wore it. He's got them all scared of him. Slept after dinner till four. Wash and shave. Played skittles after tea. Alert at 7.40 PM. Terrific barrage. Over at 8.20. Played more skittles afterwards. Bed 11.20 PM.

Sunday 16th January 1944

Up 8.5 AM. Home 9.45 AM. Slept after breakfast until 12.30 PM. Read after dinner. Changed brakes on cycle. (Still thick fog today.)

Monday 17th January 1944

Worked on wall this morning. This afternoon, Martin had the men walking round picking up bits of wood; always looking out of the window at them. Somebody scratched on the wall, 'Willy Regan goes out with Nelly Bracken'. I let it stay. Men arrived to erect telegraph pole. File main-spring spindle of clock to fit square key. Bert Forbes mending a watch for Mrs. Warren, finds it is one he was unable to do for Martin. Martin apparently sold it to her. What a <u>man</u>! Letter came from Avery, on board ship; Barden gave me a 10 ore piece this evening: Denmark 1876. Skittles after tea. I won the last game of 5, being 2d out. Won a game of 31s. 10 halfpenny. Bed 10.50 PM.

Tuesday 18th January 1944

Up 7.00 AM. Put 6d on savings. Home 10.0 AM. Cleaned 2 cantilevers. Out to Catford this afternoon. Vi went to the pictures this evening. Joan went dancing. Vi to the Brownies.

Thursday 20th January 1944

Home at 8.35 AM. Read all morning, dug in the garden this afternoon. Vi and the kids had just gone to bed when the warning went. At 9.50 PM. All Clear at 10.05 PM. Earlier this evening, Joan brought a friend in, and with little Vi, and I, acted a play that Joan fondly hopes to stage.

Friday 21st January 1944

Depot at 8.15 AM. Martin not in today, in consequence after dinner the rest went to bed, as they should. I did no work all day, but spent the time making a wooden pillow, and fixing a plug and socket on to the electric fire, so that I may have either the light or the fire, or both, on or off, as I please. Went to library, and got 4 books, one a spy story, another a romance, and for Joan. *Just William*, the fourth. *Roman Britain*.

After tea, billiards, warning went at 8.40 PM., while our planes were exercising; appeared to be a heavy raid, or an attempt at it. Most terrific barrage I've ever heard, lasted for half an hour continuously at one period. All Clear about 10.10 PM. Played skittles, then to bed at 11.05 PM., to read until 12.45 PM. Awoke at 4.10 AM, by voices at the door of my shelter, then I found the warning had gone ten minutes before; by the time I had my jacket and boots on, the barrage was in full swing, if anything, it was even more intense than the earlier raid, and continuous for nearly an hour. Flares dropped. Fires could be seen towards Walthamstow, and Dartford. Ted Bennett rang up after the earlier raid to say that quite a few of our own shells had fallen in his district, doing some damage. (Brewery at Romford.)

Saturday 22nd January 1944

Home 9.45 AM. Haircut at Greenwich. Made the beds while Vi did the shopping. She got 4 eggs today (wonders will never cease!) Slept this afternoon. Letter from the fellow who is buying the motorcycle, full of complaints about its condition, and offers me £6.

Sunday 23rd January 1944

Depot 9.00 AM. One of the window-sashes of the sleeping quarters blown out by the wind last night. A-Shift didn't trouble to pick it up, so Alf Crawley began to repair it, and Blundell came along and suggested that it be 'spiked' in position. What a suggestion, what brilliance! Never a constructive suggestion. The quarters were junk, and jerry-built from the start. Found a wood-chisel, marked 1111, under a palliasse. Montcalm this evening. Bed at 8.00 PM. Up at 6.15 AM. Back to depot 7.30 AM.

Monday 24th January 1944

Home at 9.00 AM. Dug in the garden. After dinner made another black-out shutter for the kids' room. Made up club account.

Tuesday 25th January 1944

Depot at 8.10 AM. Martin not back yet. (Hooray). Spent the morning sifting baked sand through a sand-bag. Bracken got a new pair of boots. After dinner. Tyler said <u>somebody</u> was coming down, so he would have to make them work, instead of resting, as they should. They wore it, the spineless lot. Went out through the power-house at 3.30 to go to the library. Played snooker after tea. Policeman found a pair of bolt-croppers about 5.00 PM. Threw them over the depot wall. I took them up to Tyler. He said, if they were not missing from our tools, he would keep them, or as he said, "Find a home for them." So I suppose whoever has lost them must suffer for it, while Tyler is a pair of bolt croppers to the good. Montcalm at 6.30 P.M, bed at 10.00 PM.

Wednesday 26th January 1944

Up 6.15 AM. King went at 7.00 AM. Back to depot 7.30 AM. Home at 8.50 AM. Dug in the garden, until it rained after dinner. Slept this afternoon. Read this evening.

Thursday 27th January 1944

Depot 8.5 AM. Spent all day sifting sand. Pay clerk gave me 15/- to pay for my glasses. Montcalm this evening. Kingsbridge for a couple of-drinks with Wright and Bracken. Wilson back today.

Friday 28th January 1944

Back to depot at 7.15 AM. Home at 8.45 AM. Home Guard papers came for me. Dug in the garden after dinner. Put fence posts back to their proper position. Next door neighbours had apparently been moving them to get more ground. Stan came about 3.30 PM, stayed to tea. Went to the King Alfred with Vi. Saw Stan off, and when I got back, put the wireless on, and almost immediately it went off 10.10, warning 10.25. Distant gunfire. All Clear 11.15 PM.

HEAVY RESCUE SQUAD WORK ON THE ISLE OF DOGS

Saturday 29th January 1944

Depot 8.10 AM. Bridge. Forbes and Barden also. Did a little work on window openings. Slept after dinner, until 5.00 PM. Playing skittles after tea, warning went at about 8.20 PM. Barrage very heavy, but did not appear to be as heavy as last Friday. Dropped a few bombs somewhere handy, caused a large fire to the north of us. After the All Clear, went to the George with Forbes. Should have met Stan, but he was not there. Found out the fire was at Poplar High St. Tyler said no incident for us. About 5.15 AM, heard a lorry go out; came back about 15 mins later, went out again. George Pryor woke me at 6.15 AM. I and Bill Bracken were to go out with Pryor's gang to High St. Barden had already gone. We were to go at 8.00 AM. The lorry I had heard, was Barden's gang going to the job, and returning for gum-boots, as water was to be worked in.

Tyler told the 3 part-timers, they need not go out on the job, as they had to go to their own work, and they could go home at 7.0 A.M, they get 3/- per night for 12 hours, and go home next morning at 5.00 AM. One of them (a milkman), said he wouldn't go out on the incident in any case, as he said he'd got to start work early. Drafted in the Service, but don't intend to do the job. Tyler sides with them.

Went to the High St, at 7.50 AM. Block of flats blasted and burnt out, between Bow Lane and Newby Place. We were to recover the body of an 8 month old baby. Barden's gang had already done this, so we were to demolish an overhanging piece of masonry. Pryor, with Wood, myself, and Balls and Ginsberg went up to tie a rope round it. Wood and I secured it. It was demolished very neatly. George Pryor was pleased, so was Tyler. We don't like to have any slips, it looks and makes us feel incompetent.

Some more overhanging brickwork had to come down, so we five went up again. Ginsberg endeavoured to jar it down with a length of timber, as there was no other way of reaching it. The foothold for us was <u>very</u> precarious, and that timber being so long and heavy. Ginsberg could hardly reach it. As Pryor was leader, he was saying to 'Taffy' Ginsberg, in a quiet voice, and the proper manner. "Little higher Taffy," and "Up a bit," etc, as the occasion demanded. Tyler, in the high-pitched querulous voice he has, began to scream, (scream is the only way to describe it) "No, no, no, up higher, not there, up higher." I said to George P. "Tell him to shut up, he's unnerving the man." So George called out to Tyler, "Come up here yourself and see if you can do it, you old c...." It could not be done, so George P, got a ladder and stood it against a steel joist, while he and Taffy stood on the foot. I mounted to the top, took a floorboard, which was light enough to wield, and disposed of that little job. We came down, and had a cup of tea, and a few biscuits from the mobile canteen, presented by 'Gert and Daisy' to Poplar. While drinking the tea, a woman still suffering from shock, came and asked us if we could get her to the flat to salvage some of her belongings. Tyler took her away and came back with her a few minutes later, saying he couldn't get her to her flat. Alf and I said we could manage it, so Tyler said, "Alright, see what you can do for her." We did, we got a fireman's short ladder, split it, and had one section each side of a wall for her to get over and back. As we were coming back. Tyler started shouting while we were some way off, and in consequence, the firemen, and spectators looked to see what the naughty boys were doing. Alf said to me, "Hark at him Bill, he makes you all look as if you had done something wrong. I'm going to speak to somebody about him tomorrow." When I got up to Tyler I said to him, "Were you shouting at me?" He said "Yes, we've got to go back, and you are holding us up." So I said he should be ashamed of himself, shouting like he does, and making us look like a lot of fools, and told him that the other men about, were laughing at us, and taking the 'p...' out of us. He got angry, but said nothing, for which I was glad, as I was in no good mood; back to the depot at 9.00 AM. Told we need not come in until 9.0 AM. Monday morning.

(I believe there are more casualties on this incident, but nobody seems to know for certain.)

HEAVY RESCUE SQUAD WORK ON THE ISLE OF DOGS

Sunday 30th January 1944

Home at 10.0 AM. Breakfast; took Joan with me to see Mum. Stan and I to the Northover for a drink. Home to dinner at 2.35 p m. Charlie and Vera and her two kids came to tea tonight. We had shrimps, winkles, beetroot, cheese, jam, custard and prunes. They went at 8.00 PM.

I find that Nun was present, and reprimanded Tyler for not wearing his uniform. The 'incident' has been put in the contractors' hands already.

Monday 31st January 1944

Arrived at the depot at 9.20 AM, having caught a bridge at Glengall Grove. Lorry left as I arrived. I went to Ravely Street by bus. Concreting. After dinner, to Manchester Rd. Found the frame of a doll's pram, brought it back, and will take it home. Went to the library at 4.30 P.M, and to Haffkin's about my glasses. Not ready yet. Met Pryor on the way back, and went to the Pin with him, where King. Bird and Page already were, until 6.30 PM. After tea snooker, to the Pin with Forbes and Wood.

Tuesday 1st February 1944

Home at 9.40 AM. With wire for garden fence, and meat for cats. Read until dinner-time *They Die with Their Boots Clean*. Slept after dinner. Overhauled cycle; read a little to Little Vi. Mended Joan's pump. Washed up the dishes.

Wednesday 2nd February 1944

Depot 8.10 AM. Manchester Rd, this morning. Afternoon work in the depot. Played skittles and billiards after tea, bed 11.15 p m.

Thursday 3rd February 1944

Home at 8.45 A.M, with tea-tray. Worked in garden all morning. Slept this afternoon. Stan came about 4.00 P.M, stayed to tea. Saw him off at 7.30. Alert at 8.40 for about half an hour. Heavy barrage but apparently very few raiders. Shove-ha'penny with Little Vi. Bed 11.00 PM.

Friday 4th February 1944

Up at 5.00 AM. Alert heavy raid, but appeared to be widespread. Lasted about an hour. Lighted fire, cup of tea and toast for Vi. Depot at 8.05 AM. Barden not in. His gang to Maria St. Ginsberg and Page and Balls, can rest. Bracken and I cut up firewood for billiard room, while King's in doing the women's work in the canteen.

This afternoon to Manchester Rd., where we lighted a fire, to burn up some rubbish. King has done the thing that a man in his position should never do. About 2.45 PM, Bracken said to King, "Bill and me are going to have a cup of tea, alright?" King said, "Fuck you, do what you fucking-well like. I don't care what you do." When Bracken asked what was the matter with him, King rushed at Bracken and pushed him violently in the chest with both hands, and if Bracken had not been holding on to the door-way, he would have fallen backwards down a heap of hard-core, and certainly been injured. It appears to have begun over Bracken not speaking to King in the depot. I told Bracken to report the matter, but he doesn't seem inclined to. King has tried some funny stuff with me, before, and I would prefer not to be in his gang. He licks Tyler and Martin's boots, and allows them to swing all the 'dirty' jobs on to Bracken and I.

To the library on the way back. After supper, to the Pin with Forbes.

Saturday 5th February 1944

Home at 9.00 AM with firewood. Dug in garden all morning. After dinner. Vi and the kids to the 'Pics'. Stan came this afternoon, and we played shove-ha'penny till 5.00 PM. Saw him to the trams. Reading and writing this evening.

Sunday 6th February 1944

Alert at 5.55 A.M, so up and made a pot of tea and lighted fire; All Clear about 6.00 AM. Depot at 9.10 AM. Had to get a new fuse put in, as Tuting had blown it. Charlie came at 4.45 PM. He had two games of Billiards and while I was washing, he went. He brought my watch back, the fellow he had given it to could not do it and had put the works back wrongly. Also, the loose silver dust cover is missing. To the Pin with Forbes.

Monday 7th February 1944

Up 6.50 AM. Home 9.15 AM. In the garden all morning, and chopped wood. Vi and the kids went to Mother's last night, to tea. Vi tells me that Dorrie wants me to make a cot for her coming baby. Dug a little in garden this afternoon. Read this evening, and treated my feet.

Tuesday 8th February 1944

Depot 8.10 AM. Martin in today, worse luck. Bracken and I re-sheeted the lorry, and checked tools, and lowered the seat. Martin and/or Tyler had Ginsberg and Balls sweeping the puddles away. What a useless pastime. Give the men some constructive work, instead of making them look ridiculous. To Manchester Rd, after dinner. Back to the library. Billiards and snooker after tea. To the Pin with Forbes. Bed at 11.00 PM to read for an hour. This noon, found electric cable for dug-outs and control, lying on the ground broken by A-Shift again. Mended it.

Wednesday 9th February 1944

Up at 7.00 AM. Nunn and Roberts came at 7.50 AM. Home with about 100 ft, of electric light wire. Dug in garden. After dinner limed garden, and used wire to stop the cats getting on the garden. Read this evening, and got electric light socket out for Tuting and Forbes tomorrow.

Thursday 10th February 1944

Depot. Manchester Rd, today. After dinner, found electric light socket had been stolen from my shelter. Told Tyler of it, and he says he can't do anything about it. That I was allowed the light for compassion. Martin poked his nose in, and I told him I was 'not talking to him', and when I went out, he started shouting and swearing, so I came back, and told him not to swear at me, as I would have him stopped. Repaired electric fire after tea. To the Pin with Forbes. Bed 10.45 PM.

Friday 11th February 1944

Up 7.00 AM. Home 9.00 AM. Loafed about all day. Alert this evening. Heavy barrage again, as is becoming usual.

Saturday 12th February 1944

Depot 8.10 AM. Fixed electric light in gatekeeper's hut, also in control room. Library this evening. Alert at 8.50 until 9.30 PM. To bed after All Clear.

Sunday 13th February 1944

Home 9.30 with 1 pint of winkles. Bath after dinner. Charlie came to tea about 4.15, and brought me a blue suit. I gave him a page of coupons for it. To the Fellowship with him at 7.10 P.M, until the Alert at 8.35 PM. Came home through barrage. Vi waiting at the door. Shell splinters fell very thickly tonight. All clear about 9.30 PM.

Monday 14th February 1944

Up 7.15 AM. Phoned depot I could be late. Got in at 8.55 AM. Gang gone to get cement. (15 cwt.) King not in. Passmores brought sand and cement. Made 1 louvre for control-room. Manchester Rd, this afternoon. 1 lorry. Went for my glasses at 4. They don't suit at all. Read, and played snooker all evening. Bed 10.30.

Tuesday. 15th February 1944

Up 6.15 AM. Had first cup of tea at 6.25. Shaved washed. No more tea after 7.00 AM. None of the women turned up. Home 9.00 AM. Worked in garden all morning. Slept all afternoon. Read all evening.

This morning Martin told us, we would be going on gas drill and decontamination tomorrow.

HEAVY RESCUE SQUAD WORK ON THE ISLE OF DOGS

Wednesday 16th February 1944

Depot 8.00 AM. King in today. Barden goes to decontamination, not us. We to Manchester Rd., it rained continuously. A useless procedure to send men out in weather like this. Bracken not in.

Thursday 17th February 1944

Home at 9.00 AM. Loafed about all day.

Friday 18th February 1944

Depot 8.00 AM. Decontamination 9.30 - 11.30 AM. A useless procedure. We had to dress in gas suits. We were exempted from work this afternoon, but King came to tell me that Tyler had said we were to saw wood for the fire. I would not, but went to sleep instead.

After tea snooker and billiards. Bed 10.15 PM. Alert at 12.45 AM until 1.40 AM. Heavy barrage, and five fires could be seen from the depot, 3 to the west, and to the north. 1 to the east.

Saturday 19th February 1944

Home 9.00 AM. Helped with the housework. Bed after dinner until 5.00 PM. Joan and Vi, to a party next door. Wrights. Read all evening.

Sunday 20th February 1944

Depot 9.10 AM. Loafed about all day. Had no tea; while King hangs over the bar of the canteen. I will not go near. A pity he is not as efficient a leader as he is at scrimping with the food.

Alert at 9.30; heavy barrage, and lots of planes. All clear at 10.40 PM. Some fires to the north, east, and south of west. Awoke at 3.30 AM. Another alert, but nothing materialised. All clear 4.00 AM. Andrews took Martin, his woman, and Barden to Stepney, in Light Rescue car, and smashed themselves up, near Stepney Station.

BILL REGAN'S DIARY FROM THE SECOND WORLD WAR

Monday 21st February 1944

Home 9.10AM and dug in garden. After dinner, read for a while, chopped firewood. Bag-full for Mum at 5.00 PM. Gave me two lemons. Tells me she and Dorrie would have gone back to Chipping Norton, through the raids, if it were not for Ken.

Back home 6.25 PM. Read all evening. Bed 10.45 PM. Up again at 3.00 AM. Alert. Gunfire distant. All clear 3.40 AM. Made tea, and back to bed at 4.10 AM.

(H.E., and incendiaries were dropped where Mum lives).

Tuesday 22nd February 1944

Up 7.15, to depot at speed, at 8.10 AM. I find that Martin has his nose and face cut up, a pity it wasn't worse. Barden has broken leg, and arm, and his face cut. Charlie Andrews a black eye, the woman apparently uninjured. This should be the finish of Martin. (We all hope, except two, Rushby and Wilson.)

Manchester Rd, this morning and afternoon. Yet we are supposed to rest during the afternoon; we are messed about, but nobody will back up my protests. Played billiards and snooker this evening. To the Pin with Forbes at 9.35 PM. Awoke to find Forbes and Tuting sitting on my bed. Alert had been sounded, but I had not heard. A really terrific barrage was put up. Appeared to be a very heavy concentration of raiders. All clear 1.40 AM.

Wednesday 23rd February 1944

Up 7.20. Pumped Forbes' near tyre and burst the connection. The second one in 10 days. I must get him another. Home at 10.15 AM. Read until dinner. Slept after dinner until 3.30. After tea, filled a bottle with petrol, for Forbes. Read all evening. Had half a lemon this evening. Vi and the kids to bed at 9.30 PM. Alert at 10.00 PM. After about 10 minutes a terrific barrage. Appeared to be about 10 or 12 raiders at a time, in waves, dropped plenty of phosphorus bombs in the direction of the City. All Clear 11.15 PM. (Had a letter from Doncaster today, urging me to send Vi and the kids up there while the raids last. I hope Vi goes. Bed 11.25 p m. I suppose there will be another alert before morning.

Thursday 24th February 1944

Depot 8.05 AM. Manchester Rd, this morning. Hard core lorry had to wait until we demolished a wall before we could give him a load. After dinner and before we were paid. Martin said he wanted to see me. I asked, "When?" He said before you go out again. I reminded him that the order was, rest for half a day after a raid. He said he would get on the phone for confirmation. He should not need to, the order was clear enough. Anyway, later on, he told Lewington that he had done that, and that Town Hall had said we were to go to work. I don't believe it. Needless to say. I would not work. After tea, went to Mellish St, and invited the soldiers billeted there to use our sports' facilities. About 8.15 AM. 2 of them came over; I paid 6d halfpenny for their refreshment. While they were playing snooker at about 9.35 P.M, the Alert sounded. It developed into a heavy raid. F.B.[1], dropped behind the Vulcan at Deptford Ferry St., set light to a stack of timber, and made a blaze that lasted all night. All clear about 11.00 PM.

Friday 25th February 1944

Home 9.15 AM. Discussed with Vi, the desirability of sending her and the kids to Doncaster. Nothing settled. Bought 2 pre-war bicycle pump connectors at Haywards Garage.

Saturday 26th February 1944

Depot 8.5 AM. Manchester Rd, again this morning. After dinner, read a little, slept until 4.40 PM. After tea billiards and snooker. Bed 10.10 PM. Wright not in. Paid for 2 lots of refreshment for soldiers - 1/-.

---

[1] Fire Bombs

Sunday 27th February 1944

Home 9.30 A.M, with a pint of winkles. Charlie not coming to dinner and tea as promised. Vi showed me a letter from Mrs. Harris, who wants us to send the kids back to Lidstone. I think we will. Joan wants to go, and Vi and I persuaded little Vi so that at the finish she was busy making a list of articles to take with her. To Downham to see Mum, at 9.05 PM. Arrived at 9.45 PM. Mum agrees that we should send them back. Walked back home, arrived 10.50 PM.

Monday 28th February 1944

Depot 8.05 AM. King not in, nor Wright. To Manchester Rd After dinner Manchester Rd., where I left the gang and went to Bancroft Rd., to pay 7/6d, also to see about the re-evacuation of the kids. That can be done, but must pay the fare this time. Back to Manchester Rd, at 3.45, and immediately to the library, and from there to Maria St, to pick up firewood for the depot fires. After tea snooker. After supper Forbes and I and 2 soldiers played snooker. To the Pin at 9.40 PM with one of them. Bed 10.45 PM.

Tuesday 29th February 1944

Home 8.50 AM. Joan not well enough to go to school. Told Vi about evacuation. Joan says she doesn't want to go now. Vi said nothing. Read all morning. Slept this afternoon. Joan got up at 4.00 PM and went out on her cycle. Read this evening, and helped little Vi with her homework. She doesn't need help, and I believe she asks me to help, so that she can show me how clever she is. Alert 9.30 P.M, usual barrage, and seemed to be about half a dozen planes. Bomb dropped somewhere on the hill, close by. 9.40. All clear 10.00 PM.

Wednesday 1st March 1944

Depot 8.10 AM. King not in again. To Manchester Rd. To the library, and Depot 4.00 PM. Alert at 12.30 AM. Last about 50 minutes. Usual heavy barrage. Five fires could be seen, to the East, and South.

HEAVY RESCUE SQUAD WORK ON THE ISLE OF DOGS

Thursday 2nd March 1944

Home 10.00.AM. Vi said an A.A. shell had landed. 5 doors away, shook them up somewhat, so she put the kids under the stairs. Sawed firewood up, and took it to Mum at Downham. Mum says she will lend us the money to take the kids' back to Oxford. Slept this afternoon. Read all evening. Bed 10.15 p m.

Friday 3rd March 1944

Depot 8.15 AM. Bridge at Glengall Grove. Manchester Road this morning. This afternoon. Lewington said he would be back to depot at 4.00 PM. I asked King at 3.52 PM if he was going back, he said it was too early. To the library, back to depot. 4.15 PM. Lewington had been back some time before us.

After tea, billiards and snooker, with Forbes and two soldiers. To the Pin. Bed 10.45 PM.

Saturday 4th March 1944

Home 9.30 AM. Vi posted letter to Lidstone. Joan has a cold on her chest. Shopping with Vi this morning. To Lewisham this afternoon to get underclothes for the kids. Shoes for Joan. Read all evening. Bed 11.50 PM. Made up Club books.

Sunday 5th March 1944

Up 7.10 AM. Made tea, and went back to bed. Vi trying to scratch the cat's ear, spilt her tea all over the bedclothes. Depot 9.10 AM. Repaired two black-out curtains in the canteen. Bracken half shift off. After dinner, wrote to Doncaster. Laid down for a while. Snooker and billiards after tea, bed 10.30 PM.

Monday 6th March 1944

To Lenanton's with Fred Wood, to start work part-time at 1/10d farthing per hour. Did not do much, but Wood said it was his busiest day since he had been there. Home 6.00 PM. Vi not sending the kids away Wednesday, as Little Vi has got a cold now.

John Lenanton's Timber Firm, Westferry Rd.[1]

Tuesday 7th March 1944

Depot 8.15 AM. Manchester Rd. Why does Martin and Tyler keep sending debris lorries to us. It gives me no time to demolish the brickwork. I am the only man to go on top now. Words with King about it, but he is too frightened to do anything about it. Called at Glengall Grove School for stores, and I went straight on to library. Walked back to depot, had bridge[2] for 25 minutes. After tea

---

[1] Photo: Island History Trust Collection
[2] Glengall Road Bridge operated hydraulically – and Bill had to wait for the bridge.

snooker with Forbes and two soldiers, whose supper I paid for. Got Andrews to mend Joan's shoes. Bed 11.00 PM.

Wednesday 8th March 1944

Up 7.20 AM. Clock had stopped. Worked same place as Monday. Home 6.15 PM with spring mattress from an old bed in the depot, will do for baby cot for Dorrie. Bracken told me his relative is sending me £9 in settlement for motor-cycle. About time too. Alert at 9.30 PM this evening, nothing happened, All Clear 10.05 PM.

Thursday 9th March 1944

Depot 8.10 AM. Manchester Rd, this morning and afternoon. Depot all evening, billiards and snooker.

Friday 10th March 1944

Lenanton's, pay day. Did a considerable amount of work. No work for Sunday, a pity, it would have made a big packet for next week.

Saturday 11th March 1944

Did not go to depot today. Vi went to Chrisp St, also got a certificate from Dr. Blasker, and a form for priority milk for me. To Mum's this evening, so that the kids could say Goodbye before going away. Mum. Dorrie, and Ken, each gave them some money, also an orange each for all of us. Home about 9.00 PM.

Sunday 12th March 1944

Charlie came to tea. Vi busy packing for the kids. After tea, Charlie gave Vi another £1 to help toward the fares. He and I, to the Fellowship Inn until about 9.00 PM. Alert about 10.00 PM. All Clear 10.30 PM. Nothing doing.

Monday 13th March 1944

Up early, and to Paddington. 9.45 train to Oxford arrive at 11.45. To car park. Mrs. Harris not there. Bought cup of tea for us four, and two sandwiches - 1/8. Scandalous. To the station, back to car park, found Mrs. Harris. To dinner at Marks and Spencer's. 1/7 each and good value. To get 3.40 train. 35 minutes late. Paddington about 6.10 PM. Home 7.15 p m. Awake at 1.00 AM. All Clear going, had not heard the Alert.

Tuesday 14th March 1944

Up 8.30 AM. To the Food Office. Greenwich for haircut. After dinner Food Office again. Bought tin of milk, jar of pickles. 2 pots meat paste. 4 boxes matches, got my medicine and pills. Read after tea.

Vi to bed 10.15 PM. Alert at 10.35 PM. A most terrific barrage again. Concussion of shell-bursts shakes everything. Two fires N. and N.W. of here. All Clear 11.43 PM.

Wednesday 15th March 1944

To Downham this afternoon. Read all evening. Alert 9.10 PM. Not so heavy as last night.

Thursday 16th March 1944

Stayed in all day. Letter from the kids.

Friday 17th March 1944

To the depot for pay. Sent £2.1.6, to Bancroft Rd. Paid Wilson club and billiards money. Paid £1 deposit off cot for Dorrie. To Downham. Home 6.00 PM.

Saturday 18th March 1944

To Chrisp St, Blasker, back to Catford, then home to dinner. To Downham this afternoon. Dorrie and I to Lewisham to get cot. Shop shut. Home to tea with D. Vi and I with Dorrie to Downham, home about 8.45 PM. Letter from Stan.

Sunday 19th March 1944

To work at Lenanton's. Home 5.45 PM. Got ready to go out, went to the top of the street and came back. Bed 10.15 PM.

HEAVY RESCUE SQUAD WORK ON THE ISLE OF DOGS

Monday 20th March 1944

Lenanton's again today. Home 6.00 PM.

Tuesday 21st March 1944

Home all day. Wrote letter to Stan. Bed 10.50 PM. Alert 12.55 PM. Heavy barrage again. About 6 fires, all over the place. Saw many phosphorous bombs coming down in every direction. Raiders appeared to come in together. All Clear 1.55 AM. Three large fires still burning. E, and 2 N, approx. 1 Woolwich. 2 towards Bermondsey and Elephant. Made tea, bed 2.15 AM.

Wednesday 22nd March 1944

Up 8.30 AM. Cleaned up in the house, while Vi was out. Went to Downham this evening. Stayed to tea. Home 7.45 PM. Alert at 9.20 PM. Usual heavy barrage. Shell splinters particularly thick round here tonight. Only a few raiders over. All Clear 9.55 PM.

Thursday 23rd March 1944

Out on cycle 10.00 AM. Saw where bomb dropped in the ground of Greenwich College. Bought pair of pedals at Deptford. On to Tower Bridge. Waterloo. Borough. Elephant. Old Kent Rd. Deptford. Lewisham, and to Beckenham: home 3.55 PM.

Friday 24th March 1944

To the Island, to get my money from Lenanton's. Money not arrived. To Stepney. Back to Island, home about 3.00 PM. Stayed in all evening.

Alert about 10.20, raid developed about 11.10 PM. Definitely the biggest effort our barrage has ever made; continuous for approx. 50 minutes. All Clear about 1.20 AM. Vi got up 1.00 AM.

Saturday 25th March 1944

To the Island. Met Tyler in West Ferry Road. He told me Bracken had phoned to say his house had got it last night. Tyler says, "Only King in the gang now." Wright, the driver is still out. Got my money from Lenanton's. To Dr. Blasker, who says I have a touch of pleurisy. Gave me a letter to take to Saint John's Hospital, for examination and X-ray. Home, about 3.30 PM after watching football, with my medicine and Kaolin Poultice. Read all evening. Letter from the kids' today, like their new school, and mates. Panel- money, but only 1 week.

Sunday 26th March 1944

Up about 9.00 AM. Worked in the garden. After dinner slept awhile. More gardening. Charlie came to tea. Out to the Fellowship with Charlie and Vi. Met Jack Mable and his wife. Stayed until nearly 10.00 PM.

Monday 27th March 1944

Up and to St. John's Hospital. Got back at 2.00 PM. Saw Dr. Ashton, who examined me, and says, "No pleurisy. Bronchitis – yes." X-rayed. Home 5.00 PM. Letter from Stan today.

Tuesday 28th March 1944

Vi to Chrisp St. I to Elmers End to look at Bill Bracken's house. A few shattered windows, some broken tiles. Home about 12.00 midday. Gave 9d to Roman Catholic sisters. Bought a couple of rock plants home with me. Vi home about 12.30. After dinner to Catford for some plants. Spent 3/- on them 4/- for bean poles. I lined up for 2lbs of oranges. Planted flowers in garden, back and front. Read all evening.

Wednesday 29th March 1944

Up 8.20 AM. Vi to Catford market. I to Catford to get 2 more flower plants. After dinner, dug in front garden.

4.00 PM to Downham with cot for Dorrie, and tea. Home at 7.00 PM and watered garden. Read *Strange Conflict*.

Thursday 30th March 1944

Up 3.30 AM. Alert until 4.00 AM. Flares, little gunfire. To bed, up again 8.45 AM. In the garden all day. Read all evening.

Friday 31st March 1944

Up 8.00 AM. Vi to depot to get money. I for a walk to Catford. In the garden this evening. To the King Alfred until 10.00 PM.

Saturday 1st April 1944

To see Blasker. Watched football this afternoon. Did a bit more to the garden. Read this evening.

Sunday 2nd April 1944

Did more to front garden. Beanpoles in the back. Vi sowed peas. Read all evening.

Monday 3rd April 1944

Up 9.00 AM. In all morning. For medicine 1.00 PM. Vi to buy coat this afternoon. To Downham this afternoon and evening. I stayed home. Dominoes later this evening.

Saturday 8th April 1944

Vi to Dr. Blasker, for certificate. I to Kings X to meet Mr., Mrs, and Mary Embley[1]. Arrived 1.12 PM. Home 3.15 PM. They brought plenty of food, and about 2lb of cheese for me. To the 'King Alfred' after tea.

Sunday 9th April 1944

(At home all day) Len and Hilda, and Mary to Gillingham to see Ron who is in detention camp for 112 days[2]. Home 7.30 PM. To the 'King Alfred' after 8.0 PM.

---

[1] Doncaster friends.
[2] Ron Embley in detention for being absent without leave.

Monday 10th April 1944

Len. Mary and I, to Blackheath, saw rocket-gun battery, to Greenwich Park, showed them Observatory. Meridian Line. 2 drinks in the 'Admiral Hardy', looked at Seamen's Hospital, which has been blasted again. To the Island, met Blasker in Stebondale St, about an hour in the George. To the Depot at 3.00 PM. Len and I played billiards. Had our tea bought for us by Alf Crawley. Home 5.50 PM. Vi and Hilda to Downham, we followed later, and had supper there. To the Albion at Lewisham. Posted panel certificate at Greenwich 1.00 PM.

Tuesday 11th April 1944

Len and I to post parcel to the kids, to the Fellowship until 3.00 PM. Tram to the Oval, another to Westminster. Through to Abbey to Broadway' coffee shop to the George for a drink. (Queen Anne's Gate.) St. James Park,

Buckingham Palace, Green Park, walked from Piccadilly to Fleet St. Cup of coffee. Ludgate Hill. St. Paul's, to Cannon St and London Bridge. 47 Bus home, at 8.50 PM. Vi and Hilda to the Albion, we followed. Met Ernie Burton. Home 10.50 PM.

Wednesday 12th April 1944

All of us by tram to Blackfriars Bridge. Walked down Lower Thames St to the Monument, but it was closed. Cannon St, dinner, drinks. To St. Paul's to the Whispering Gallery and dome. Crypt. Fed pigeons in Trafalgar Sq. Admiralty Arch, to the Palace, same coffee shop at Broadway. Alert about 12.30 not much activity.

Thursday 13th April 1944

Quiet day today. Hilda and Vi too tired after yesterday's walking. I to Parks at Catford, to get cable for near brake, had to wait for it to be done. Back to King Alfred home 10.30 PM. Alert about 1.00 PM, rather more activity.

Friday 14th April 1944

Vi and Hilda to the Island. Len. Mary and I at home. Vi back at 4.30 PM. I gave Len 3 1bs sugar, half a pound of tea, pair of brown shoes. Mary drawing ruler, and camera. After tea. King Alfred.

Saturday 15th April 1944

Vi at home. I to King's Cross with Len. Hilda, and Mary. 1.25 train. Home at 3.30 PM. Vi out, back at 4.30 PM. Stayed home this evening. No panel money yet.

Sunday 16th April 1944

Depot 9.00 AM. Blundell started as soon as I got in. He wanted sick certificate. I told him he was unlucky. Met Dr. Blasker at depot gate at 11.30 AM. He came into the gatekeeper's hut, told me I was not fit for work. Gave me a letter for M.O.H. (L.C.C.) Certificate for Town Hall, and I to call for final panel certificate this afternoon, which I did. Billiards and snooker, to the Pin with Forbes. Bed in the sleeping quarters.

Monday 17th April 1944

Up 6.45 AM. Home all day. Nothing of note. Yesterday, posted panel certificate to M.O.H, by mistake. Wrote to him, asking him to return it. No panel money yet.

Tuesday 18th April 1944

Depot 8.05 AM. Manchester Rd this morning. Afternoon with Wilson. Martin, instructing Light Rescue in singlestick[1]. I let Wilson do it. He's crawling for Barden's job, but can't even use scaffold hammer, or tie. Left fall rope out. What a game!!! Slept in

---

[1] Using single pole as crane or lift to help someone down from damaged building

the quarters again. Alert 1.30 AM. Fixed fire and light in shelter, and shall sleep there again in future. Rather heavy barrage, now that Len and Hilda have gone back.

Wednesday 19th April 1944

Home 9.15 AM. Home all day. To Downham to tea, borrowed book from Ken, lent him one. Home 9.15 p m.

Thursday 20th April 1944

Depot. 8.05 AM. In all morning. Instructing Light Rescue this afternoon, using club hammer and cold chisel. Vi came after tea, with form to fill in, for job in Royal Army Pay Corps. Tyler signed it. To the Pin with Forbes. Saw Vi to bus, back to Pin. Bed 11.00 PM.

Friday 21st April 1944

Home 9.15 AM. In all morning, pictures this afternoon with Vi, and Iris. *Snow White*. Alert 10.25 PM. All Clear 10.55 PM. No Incidents.

Saturday 22nd April 1944

To Manchester Rd this morning, got stair nails for taking home. Helped Carlile clean cycle. After tea, billiards and snooker. To the Pin with Forbes. Were treated by Welsh-accented woman. Bed 11.15 PM. After winning one game of 31s.

Sunday 23rd April 1944

Home 10.00 AM. Beautiful day. Out on cycle into Kent. Home 4.30 PM. Charlie to tea. Quiet evening. Bed 10.30 PM.

Monday 24th April 1944

Depot 8.00 AM. Nobody out today. Instructing Light Rescue in metal cutting with hacksaw. This afternoon Tyler called me up to Games Room. 8 men distempering. I looked on. Later did some bricklaying for field-kitchen. To the Library, changed 2 books for Martin. One has Ginsberg's name on it. A-Shift locked Billiards balls away. Forbes and I unscrewed hasps, played snooker, put balls away, and padlock. Bed 10.30 PM.

Tuesday 25th April 1944

Up 6.15 AM. Saw about 200 of our bombers going to France just before 8.00 AM. Home 9.00 AM. Stayed in all day.

Answered letter from H.G. Bevis, which said he had not received Sick Sheet, which I posted Easter Monday, 10th, at Greenwich. Parcel from Hilda yesterday, some clothes for the kids, 2lbs of cheese for me. £3 for Dorrie for costume and skirt, which Hilda found were worn and moth-eaten. Wrote to H.G. Bevis.

Thursday 18th May 1944

King gave us all a tea tonight. Mr. Roberts attended. Martin told all to polish the place up (as if that were possible?) as some individuals from Regional HQ, were supposed to be coming. (They were from Dagenham or Chingford, actually). Got to get back from work at 4 P.M, so that everybody could be washed and brushed, ready for visitors. (Let them see us as we actually are, and as we really are situated); it would be more to Martin and Tyler's credit to make the place more comfortable for us. I have been rather lax with this lately, so must continue from memory.

Friday 19th May 1944

Some niggling worries at the depot, as has become an almost normal feature. Have done some bricklaying for place to house field-kitchen. Martin showed me entry in log-book. Mr. Nunn says no-one to sleep in Anderson shelters, bunks to be put back. I asked him why put bunks back if they are not to be used. (No answer, or reason). It looks as if Blundell is going to get his way. Anyway, I've ignored it, and still sleep there. Talk with librarian on history of Poplar, he tells me an attempt on this has long been needed. Seems to think I will tackle it. Maybe I will. Bought bicycle for Ken, from Bert Forbes. Have been out into Kent on cycle quite frequently, lately. Have been considering forming a Youth P.C.[1], and Sports Club, also cycle club. King and Anderson to be transferred to Monteith Rd. A-Shift. Dennison to Knapp Rd. B-Shift.

JUNE

T. Clary has taken over King's position. We have finished Manchester Rd, now 2 houses in Launch St.

Thursday 15th June 1944

Launch St this afternoon. Snooker this evening. To the Tooke[2] with Clary. Samways, Carlile, Andrews and Wenzal.

Tooke Arms (post-war)[3]

[1] Physical Culture.
[2] Tooke Arms, 165 Westferry Rd (spelled West Ferry Rd until the 1950s)
[3] Photo: Island History Trust Collection

Tyler announced compulsory fire watching. 3 men per night; I said I would not, and did not. (This was Tuesday 13th.) Bed 11.00 PM. Alert 11.37 PM. Gunfire immediately. One machine passed over from S.E, to S.W, as I got out. Searchlight held it, flying very low and fast. Every type of gun, opened up, but it seemed unaffected. One pack of rockets from Rotherhithe surrounded it, but it just veered right as if from blast, and continued toward the city. Seconds later, the engine ceased, it dived, and immediately a terrific white flash was seen. After a lapse of about 6 seconds a big red flash, and a terrific explosion.[1]

We congratulated the Ack-Ack to each other, and counted one plane down.

Immediately, another came over, held by searchlights, and surrounded by shell-bursts; as before, right through it, over-head, and going towards Poplar, as I thought. Burdett Rd; as before, the engine cut out, it dived steeply, big white flash, pause, huge red flash, bang. We felt the blast distinctly. That's two planes, we said. They seemed to be small fast fighters, with an apparently outsize bombload. Just about here, Martin who had varnished his tonsils with his usual double Scotches, got very talkative, and tried to bolster himself with loud talk. "I'm with you lads, first to go out.

---

[1] It was Bill's first sight of a V-1 rocket. Frequently referred to as the Doodlebug or Flying Bomb, the V-1 was an abbreviation of Vergeltungswaffe-1 (the German for Weapon of Revenge or Retribution), notable for the sound of its pulse jet engine and the eerie silence when that engine stopped and the rocket made its descent. Flying at 640 km/h (400 mph), it carried its 850 Kg explosive warhead from Dutch, Belgian and French launch sites to London and the South East. The first V-1 to fall on England was at 4.25 a.m. on 13th June 1944, hitting a railway bridge in Grove Road near Mile End Road. The bridge and railway track were badly damaged and a number of houses were destroyed. Six were killed, 30 injured, and more than 200 people made homeless

I'll be there." etc, etc. Before he could impress us, another one came over, passed, went silent, dropped, same white flash, pause - red flash, bang. I said to Alf Crawley, that the gunners were on form, three over, three down. Hardly credible.

We began to discuss the possibility of them being planes, as we could see flames coming from the tails of them, also a light in the nose. Some said rockets, as the flames did not seem to impede their progress.

Friday 16th June 1944

At about 12.45 we all had a cup of tea, and I went back to bed. Awoke about 6.00 AM, washed, and halfway through a shave, when another one came over, and I almost cut my throat trying to watch it, and shave at the same time.

Nothing on the news about the raid; at 10.00 AM. Forces news gave out, that rocket planes were used over the south of England. Periodically, throughout today, they have been coming over, but Mr. Morrison[1] says there is nothing to worry about, as he has the situation in hand, or will have as time goes by. Still, we shouldn't worry, he is O.K.

Saturday 17th June 1944

Bed 11.00 PM. Alert about 1.30 A.M, up with Wright from next door, and watched them coming in for about 2 hours, then went to sleep in armchair in front room until 4.45 AM. Made tea, washed, shaved, swept plaster up, that had fallen from ceiling.

A.A. Shells have been bursting at roof-top level, and had shaken it down. Also crack in front wall at ceiling level, right across front room. Depot at 9.00 AM. Blundell told Clary, we were to go to Launch St, and carry on with demolition work. I said I would not

---

[1] Home Secretary Herbert Morrison

while the Alert was still on. Others were too scared to refuse. After argument, he said he would leave it to Tyler. Tyler came in and asked Clary and I, would we go to work; I said definitely, no. I told him, that he knew the standing orders as well as I. During an Alert, return to depot immediately. If in the depot, stand by (in the shelter?) Then he asked me would I care to do a bit of brickwork on the field-kitchen. I said, "No." F--- the field kitchen. Later he came to tell us, we were on depot duties, we both said, No, we stand by.'" We did.

All Clear, and Lewington and Co. from Montcalm, went straight to their job at West Ferry Road. The fools. Find that one of these machines had fallen in Fern St, and had wrecked Knapp Rd depot, besides houses around. Barrett in the canteen, died in hospital. Taylor, Learner, and Gillingham, in the office, injured. Some casualties outside.

Afternoon, Fern St, one person missing, boy 15 yrs. After a couple of hours. Bracken found right hand and forearm, everything else in little pieces. Two American soldiers came to see the job. One of them gave us a cigarette. After some little talk. I gave him a piece of the bomb-casing from one of these robot-planes, or flying bombs. Back to depot to tea 6.00 PM. To the Pin with Forbes, alert went again about 9.50 PM. I had to leave a full glass of ale on the counter, and return to depot. Ted Bennett was there. He said, he had eight separate incidents at Westminster on Friday night. Bed, in my old shelter with Wright, and Ginsburg's brother, who is a sergeant in the engineers, at 11.10 PM. Slept intermittently until 7.00 AM. Alert still on.

Sunday 18th June 1944

Home 9.45 AM. Periodical alerts all day. To Mother at Downham, before dinner. Home to dinner 1.00 PM. Slept this afternoon for a few hours. Charlie came to tea, and with him to the Fellowship Inn, where we had one with Jack Mabery and his wife. Bed 10.10 Alert, up, down, up, down, oh nuts!

BILL REGAN'S DIARY FROM THE SECOND WORLD WAR

Monday 19th June 1944

Depot 8.5 AM. Alert still on from 7.00 AM.

Tuesday 20th June 1944

Home 9.00 AM. To Catford Town Hall for shelter bunks. Went to Forest Hill to get them this afternoon. Fixed shelter up, made bed in it.

Friday 23rd June 1944

Up 5.45 AM. Fairly good night. Made tea and toast, had it in shelter. 7.15 two came over minutes apart, fell at same place, top of Bellingham Hill. Depot 8.15 - 8.35. Blundell ordered us to Jeremiah St to look for lost hand-bag. (Alert still on.) (As I came in depot, one came out of the clouds above the flats, dive inside dock across Mellish St, several of us watching. Saw explosion, thought of blast, dived with bicycle for safety of lorry, too late. Caught and pushed, ears popped heard large lump falling, nothing else for some time. Parmenter got the piece that landed near us.) Some feeling over handbag. Roberts told Wright, he had not given the order, had it given to him. No hand-bag, back 12.00, dinner, pay, bed. Determined not to go out, only for casualties. Tea 6.00 PM. Alerts, on and off all evening. To the Pin. Had to leave 1 beer. Martin well oiled, wanted me to have drink with him. Saw one come over us, began to climb, dived straight for Hammond House, twisted to the right, about turn, straightened out, glided across river, landed in Blackwall Lane. (Allotments). To bed 10.15 PM. Slept until Alert. 12.00 approx, turned over went to sleep, and awoke and dozed, and - etc. Five of F. & T. Thorne's men killed in the dock by this morning's bomb.

Saturday 24th June 1944

Up 6.00 A.M, having slept right through the night. Alert 6.35 AM. Two or three came over. Home 8.45 A.M, breakfast. Bought 17' 0" of 2" x 2" for blast wall outside shelter. 5/-d. Dinner, eggs and bacon. After dinner, clad in shorts and shoes, began making blast-wall. Cup of tea in garden at 4.00 PM. Ken came over. He suggested going out in the country tonight. Vi said, "Go, take a blanket."

To Downham at 8.00 PM. Mum wouldn't let Ken go all night. Out 8.30 PM. No tea to be had. Back to the Alma. Birchwood. 1 pint Ken grapefruit 10.15 left Ken who went on home. I back to Birchwood, slept on grass-verge. (Hundreds of balloons here, circling from Gravesend to Croydon). Awoke after 12.00, general alert. Saw some go over. One came in up the Thames (From Belgium?) Awakened by some animal sniffing in my ear 4.30, and lay until 3.30 AM. To Downham, let myself in, and made tea. All Clear 6.45 AM. Took tea to Mum. Dorrie and Ken in shelter. Dorrie promptly tipped hers in her lap. Home 7.45, frying bacon and bread for breakfast. Took it to Vi in shelter. Lay there until 8.25

Sunday 25th June 1944

Depot 9.00 AM. Alerts on and off all day.

Monday 26th June 1944

Home 9.00 A.M Alert on and off all morning. Met Vi, 12.30. Dinner at Restaurant. Loafed around all day. Left at 11.00 PM. Slept at Ruxley, until 5.30. Home 6.25 AM.

Tuesday 27th June 1944

Home 6.25 AM. Depot 8.05 AM. To Dee St, to recover the bodies of 3 dead horses, and this while the Alert is still on. Our so-called superiors want dumping. Mobile canteen sent round at 11.30. Tried to sleep, unsuccessful. Wright doesn't sleep, neither does Pryor, Tuting. Bracken and several others. It's beginning to tell. Alerts on and off, all evening. To the Tooke 9.30. 2 pints, back 10.00; played 31s with Wright and Wenzel. I won 5d. To sleep before warning went again. Awake, to hear every bomb that came over. Sometimes five or six at once. Some sounded as though they were ours Wenzel said he ducked beneath the blankets several times. Peculiarly, everyone is unanimous in their dislike of these things. They make a bigger mess than his bombs ever did. Some have a different note somewhat like an outsize bee, and they have a proportionate sting. Bill Bracken told me he dreaded night-fall; Wright and Pryor have said the same. There is not one man I know, who is getting used to it; if anything, it is getting everyone down. The sound of a motor far or near, brings everyone to their feet, with no exceptions. Not only is this so in the depot, but also in the streets. Kids playing happily, grown-ups going about their affairs, next minute, the streets clearing as if by magic. You can see by their expressions, and the way they seem to go - well, sort of, 'let me get out of this'. You can feel the uneasiness. Unlike the old days, when everyone waited to help everyone else.

Wednesday 28th June 1944

Awakened after dozing for about 15 minutes or so, at about 5.30 AM. To Glengall Grove and East Ferry Rd; Post Office, wrecked, the George, six shops also. Westminster Bank and Thorne's joinery works, completely demolished. Glengall Grove. Launch St. Galbraith St, proportionately damaged by blast. (The radio tells us. 'Beware of Glass', they must mean blast.)

About a dozen Light Rescue men there, a light job, and they send for the heavy, after almost completing the job. Got two bodies out, man and wife. The woman supposed to be eight months pregnant. They had just previously been bombed out of their home at Catford. Incident closed at 7.00 AM. Barden came along, and started supervising. He's out of the service now, so perhaps he is trying to get back that way. Found what we thought was part of the engine. After Clary had pointed out what he said was the coils and condenser of a radio transmitting set, we found it was a typewriter. Home about 9.00 A.M Alerts all day. And night. Slept for a while in shelter at Ruxley Corner. Letters from the kids and Mrs. Harris. Took them to show Mum. Left Downham 10.00 PM. To Ruxley Corner, slept in fire-watchers hut for a while. Letters from the kids.

HEAVY RESCUE SQUAD WORK ON THE ISLE OF DOGS

Thursday 29th June 1944

Home 6.45 AM. Made tea and toast. Depot 8.5 AM. Tried to sleep most of the day, during alerts. Montcalm 7 times. To the Pin closed, so to the Tooke and had to get back quick. Another noisy night. No sleep. I have pain at the base of my head, cannot lay down, had to sit up all night. Pain been coming on 2 days.

Friday 30th June 1944

Home 8.30 AM. Built blast wall round entrance to shelter. In and out of shelter all day. Sky overcast, low cloud, helps these things. This morning 8.00 AM, bomb in Fenner's, opposite Montcalm. Habberley had left and gone back to Monteith, leaving no stand-by party at Montcalm.

Saturday 1st July 1944

Depot 8.10 AM. Found bomb had fallen behind depot, in Montague Meyers in the dock, yesterday afternoon about 4.30 PM. A-Shift working on site until 11.00 PM. Canteen and Sports room, and sleeping quarters all windows out.

In and out of shelters all day. To the Pin three ales and alert. Back 9.15 PM, cards with Wright and Wenzel. Bed 11.00 Sleep? My head, neck and ears too painful to move.

Sunday 2nd July 1944

Home 9.30 AM. No breakfast, early dinner, going to Bill Knight's at Ruxley, to stay the night. Charlie came with lady friend 4.00 P.M, upset arrangements, to Ruxley 6.30 PM. Cup of tea, and to Black Horse Sidcup, until 10.00 PM. Slept in Knight's shelter. Left cycle in garden of Bull.

Monday 3rd July 1944

Up 7.40 AM. Cup of tea at Auntie's, walked to Sidcup, picked up bicycle from Black Horse. Breakfast, home 11.00 AM. Met Vi 1.15; to Lewisham to buy frocks for herself and little Vi. Home. In and out of shelter. Bed 11.00 PM.

Tuesday 4th July 1944

Up 6.30 AM. Vi to work. I to pay rent; to Blasker to get certificate for yesterday. Fine day, but bombs been coming over frequently. Cut grass, gave it to Wrights for their rabbits. Put more earth round the shelter. Letter from Doncaster. Wrote reply, and letter to Stan.

Wednesday 5th July 1944

Up late. 7.40 AM. Depot 9.10 AM. Alerts on and off all day. 9.30 to Fletcher's Villas, near City Arms to remove stone mullions round bay-window, which I did. Samways removed loose slates. Back to depot, and to library to change books, which had not been done for 3 weeks. Read all afternoon. About 6.00 PM Forbes and I played snooker but after several attempts, had to give up, owing to frequency of Flying Bombs. About 8.00 PM 1 passed overhead to drop on Lenanton's (?) Played 31s - won 5d. 11.00 P.M to 12.00 - reading. (About 8.00 PM, bomb fell somewhere near Creek Rd and subway. Caused small fire behind Lovibonds, Norman Street).

Thursday 6th July 1944

Up 6.30 AM. Bomb on foreshore at Ferry St. Ferry House looks finished. Nelson, well blasted. Bancroft Rd Hospital hit, both during the night. Cut rest of the lawn, and trimmed the edges. Did not meet Vi at Lewisham, too late. To Downham, gave Mum lettuce for tea, it was rotten. Showed the letter from Doncaster, asking her to go there for a rest.

Friday 7th July 1944

Pay-clerk would not accept sick certificate. Slopped me 27/-. Alerts on and off all day. Forbes and I played snooker in bits and pieces. We are the only ones who play now. To the library this evening, alert while on the way back.

Saturday 8th July 1944

Home 9.00 AM. Weeding in garden. This afternoon, lent bicycle to Tony Dunkin for the weekend. At 5.00 PM, Vi and I to Ruxley, to Bill Knight's place. Arrive 6.00 PM, tea, bacon and tomatoes. Gave Vi a quarter pound of tea. To The Black Bull, where we spent about 27/-. Bed at 11.30. Alert while at the Bull, Knight's daughter came in, said new type of bomb was coming over. Bill and I watched some come over when we got back at 11.00 PM. One came up river. E, to W. Supper ham sandwiches.

Sunday 9th July 1944

Up 6.00 AM. Made tea for all of us. Left Vi, and Knight, wife and daughter in shelter. Depot 9.30 AM. Excuse - enemy action. Alert on and off all day. We to Montcalm, out of turn. Kingsbridge. 1 half-pint, bed 11.30 PM. Wright sold me a bunch of onions he had bought from Cleary. Gave Forbes watch. Hour hand loose. (Kiddle slept at depot all night.)

Monday 10th July 1944

Up 7.10 AM. Tea, and back to depot. Tea and sandwich at Greenwich. Home 9.15 AM. Took lettuce and spring onions to Downham this afternoon. Stayed to tea. Vi came straight from work. Dorrie going to Somerset on Friday. On way home, heard warning while in tram at Bellingham, was told bomb had dropped at Bromley Hill, which we had just left. Home about 8.30 PM. Bed 10.40 PM and Alert. Slept all night. Gave Stennett billiards money.

Tuesday 11th July 1944

Up 6.20 AM. Vi out to work first at 7.00 AM. I to depot 8.00 AM. Started brickwork for field kitchen. Warren has turned it in again. Alerts and bombs on and off all day. One on Surrey Docks Entrance, one on Deptford Power House. To Montcalm, 8.00PM. Kingsbridge 9.00 PM, 3 half-pints, the alert. Supper. 31s, bed 11.30 PM. Slept all night. No bombs over at all. To the library with Wenzell; Alert 7.40. Nothing heard.

Wednesday 12th July 1944

Up 7.00 AM. Some fell in Greenwich. One passed overhead at Catford. On and off all day. Letters from Doncaster. Mrs. Harris, and Nunn - the latter authorizing payment for 2 days I was stopped last week. Vi home 6.15 PM. Last alert before 10. Quiet night. (Swept up plaster fallen from walls. Bomb in Firhill Rd again Tuesday evening 6.15 PM. 5 killed.)

Thursday 13th July 1944

Up 6.15 AM. Vi out 7.00 AM. I at 7.20 AM. Depot 8.00. Old Blackheath Road Station, closed for years was hit. Alms-houses damaged, also Morton's. Thornes. Methodist Chapel, Glengall Grove School; some children waiting to be evacuated were injured, been blasted. Finished field-kitchen. This afternoon. Tyler woke me to tell me, that Pryor was cutting hole for chimney, as if I wanted to know. He hates to see anyone sleeping. Bomb flew over scraped past Montcalm flats, exploded on bank of Surrey Docks. Snooker with Forbes after tea. Montcalm, and Alert 7.50 PM. Kingsbridge 8.15, until 9.00. 31's until 11.00 PM.; bed. Quiet night.

Friday 14th July 1944

Up 6.00 AM. Wenzel away early. Back to Depot 7.30 AM. Greenwich 8.15 and Alert. Heard nothing. Put more earth round shelter entrance. Fixed electric light and wireless in shelter.

Bomb dropped on Tigers Head, Southend Lane, yesterday morning. Several alerts during the day. Got 26/- postal orders, stamps, and lighter fuel. Bacon and fried bread for tea. Vi home 6.15 PM.

Saturday 15th July 1944

Up 6.30 AM. Depot 8.00 AM. Helped Crawley to adjust his speed gear on his bicycle. Adjusted my own.

Sunday 16th July 1944

Up 7.00 AM. Bomb had fallen in South St. Home 9.30 AM. Wrote to the kids. Alerts during the day. Loafed around all day. Bed 11.15 PM.

HEAVY RESCUE SQUAD WORK ON THE ISLE OF DOGS

Monday 17th July 1944

Up 6.00 AM. All clear. Alert 6.40 AM, All Clear just after 7.00. Tram to Greenwich Church, heard bombs coming, decided to make for subway, and halfway downstairs when it exploded. Depot 8.10 AM. Alerts all day. Helped move rubble round shelter. Lay in the sun all afternoon. To the Pin after tea, where very little beer. Tooke, Pride, Pole, Blacksmiths, City Arms all closed.

Last night bomb heading for Dunbar House exploded in the air. One in Campbell Rd, another in Bow Rd, destroyed Light Rescue Depot. At Montcalm this evening, bomb passed overhead, fell beside Bryant and Mays, Fairfield Rd.

Tuesday 18th July 1944

Up 6.45 AM. Alert about 7.15. Waited for All Clear 8.10 AM. Straight home, at 9.00 AM, on bought bicycle, overhauled it; and it is a bargain. Alerts on and off this morning. Coffee stall, tea and spam sandwich, lib tomatoes, radishes. Bed 10.45 PM, in shelter.

Wednesday 19th July 1944

Up 6.0 A.M, back 6.01; bomb came over and fell on Robertson's Jam Factory. Depot 7.40 AM. Couple of bombs came over, I watched one coming up behind me; it went on and landed in Arbour Square, another Hanford St. Alerts on and off all day. Tyler, the dirty dog, found useless jobs for everyone, instead of letting the men seize some rest. I would not. Slept in the sun this afternoon, between alerts. Tea and snooker with Forbes. To the Tooke at 9.00 PM. High words with Tyler when we came back. He says he'll stop privilege. 31s. I won 1/5 half penny. Read in bed until alert about 2.40. Some came over close. One in the docks again. (Killed soldiers and 1 civilian about 7.00 AM. Thursday.

Thursday 20th July 1944

Up 6.30 AM. Alert. Shaved, and away at 7.55 AM. Tea and sandwich at Greenwich. As I left, alert sounded. Bomb coming over. I would not take diversion - bomb fell, engine still running on diversion road. Brushed dust off myself, and proceeded.

Immediately after, another fell almost same place. Home 8.45 AM. Alerts on and off all morning. Cleaned cycle wheels. Slept in garden for an hour. Tea and sandwich at coffee stall. Home, changed into shorts, to meet Vi. On the way saw Mum, promised to call on way back. Met Vi at Foots Cray 5.00 PM. Cup of tea and jam tart whilst waiting for her friend Reenie. To Mother's at 6.30 PM. Vi at 7.15 PM. I home at 7.40 PM.

Friday 22nd July 1944

Up 6.10 AM. Bombs still coming over. All Clear 7.10. Out 7.15 AM. Alert I did not hear at 7.20. Depot 7.45 AM. A. Shift had been out most of yesterday, and early this morning. Barwick went home with lorry keys. Phoned to say he had left keys at Maconochies. Rusby said he. Barwick had asked for me to go and pick keys up. I didn't believe it. Blundell would not take orders from Barwick. I believe he said that, merely to get me to go and get keys. I got overall and boots on but they thought I had gone. A bomb fell, which they thought was where I would be by that time. Luckily for me, I had not gone. Half-past twelve, to Brabazon St. 4 gangs already there getting in each other's way. Jolly and Frost on incident. Jolly interfering as usual. Two bodies already out, we got third. Waited for C.W.D, nearly an hour. Furniture removing. Could not do that whilst waiting, but must do it afterwards. Frost wanted to know who found body. Clary said we all did the job, or did he wish to recommend someone for a medal. Jolly was told, but said it had to go in report. Samways told Jolly he had 3 medals they could have, and he could eat the body if he liked. Barchester St to remove furniture.

Half way through. Lewington and Prior, with their gangs came along, leaving none at the depot, warning still on, bombs still coming over. We back to depot. (1 and a half hours rest, until 4.30). To Barchester St to pull down dangerous structure, and remove furniture. Find we must stay until 7.00 PM as it is thought deaf and dumb man is missing. He had left at 6.43 A.M, for work, bomb fell 5.56 AM. He turned up O.K. Back to depot 7.15 PM. Tea. 1 game snooker. Pryor to Barchester St, to look for body missing since Thursday, and incident had been closed. If not found in 2 hours, another squad to relieve him in 2 hours, and so on. How nice! Luckily. Pryor found him, and back before 10.00 PM.

31s bed 10.45 PM, read a little, bombs still coming over. We are first out tonight.

Saturday 22nd July 1944

Up 6.30 All Clear 7.40 AM. Home 8.40 AM. Vi still asleep in shelter. Worked in garden all day. Had a row. Long period of quiet until this evening. Bed 10.30 PM.

Sunday 23rd July 1944

Up 7.00 AM. All clear soon after. Out 8.25 AM. Coming out of subway alert sounded 8.40 AM. Bomb passed overhead, dropped in Amhert Rd. Read, slept, and loafed about all day. A few quiet periods. After tea, snooker. After supper, 31s. I lost 7 halfpenny. Bed and Alert 12.05. One dropped in the docks.

Monday 24th July 1944

Up 6.00 AM. All clear soon after. Away 7.55 AM. Home 8.30 AM. Dug in garden all morning. Paid insurance man 4 weeks. Paid rent, and 10/- coal. To chiropodist at Catford. Alert whilst there, couple of bombs dropped somewhere near. Home 5.50 PM. Made tea. Vi home 6.10 AM. Baked beans for tea. Pruned tomatoes, fed them. Trimmed front hedge. Took cycle to Freeman. Brownhill Road.

Tuesday 25th July 1944

Up 6.00 AM. All clear before 7.00 AM. Depot 7.50 AM. To Barchester St, to pull down dangerous structure. Nos. 1 and 2 on one lorry. No dangerous structures to be found, so Clary and Lewington, decided to work on shop, corner of Chrisp St, and Barchester St, getting the stock out. They had decided that good 'pickings' were to be had. I, and Wenzel would not touch the job. The others removed a collapsed floor, after a lot of fiddling, and proceeded to remove the stock of groceries, cigarettes, etc.

Warden named Wilsonham, came to Clary, and asked if he would drop a party wall, so that Wilsonham could get his bedroom furniture out, without risk. Clary said he would see, presently, this afternoon - perhaps. I had a look at it, came back and told Clary I could do the job myself, and should I. He had to say Yes'. Wenzel and I started to get a rope round it, and Clary came back to interfere. He had no idea of rhythm or swing. I pulled it down myself. Back to depot 12.15, after buying 10 weights from man whose shop they had been salvaging, and packet of writing-paper and envelopes. 6d. After dinner, back to Goodliffe street nearby to salvage furniture. I on the roof to remove loose slates, which Clary was not interested in, but said he might get a drink for furniture, (which he did not get). To Barchester St again, same place as this morning, until about 3.30 PM. I was given bar of soap as were the others. I offered to buy bottle of machine oil, but young lady would not accept the money, but gave me the oil. Samways helped himself to a jar of pickles.

After tea, to library with Alf Crawley. Snooker with Forbes, to the Pin with Wenzel, snooker with him about 10.00 PM. 31s until 12.00 midnight. Warning (Martin back today). Bomb at Bromley High St. We are out first again tonight.

Wednesday 26th July 1944

Up 7.00 AM. Warning until 8.20. Home 8.30 AM. Letter from Stan. Aired bedclothes, fixed electric fire, in shelter. Wireless in scullery. To Catford stamp and bread and breakfast sausage. Vi home 6.10 PM. Read all evening. Alert 10.30 All Clear shortly after. This is getting beyond a joke!!

Thursday 27th July 1944

Up 6.00 PM. All Clear. Depot 7.50 AM. Fixed stone slab beside field-kitchen. Pay. Bed after dinner. Alerts from 4.00 PM. onwards, until about 9.30 PM. Found 48 3" x 3" glazed tiles, and will take them home. To the Pin 9.45 p m. Back to shelter, played 3s with Wenzel. Wright, and P.C. Nimmo, until about 12.15

midnight, when bomb glided in and dropped close, so to bed. (Forbes gave me Vi's watch which he had cleaned and oiled.)

Friday 28th July 1944

Up 6.30 AM. Home 8.35 AM. Letters from Daisy Beeby and Charlie. Alert about 10.25 AM. Bomb dropped on Marks and Spencer's. Lewisham. Sent £1.6.0 evacuation money, and letter to Doncaster. Back home, and cut my hair. Made a sight of it. Dinner at Meals Centre. Changed into shorts, and away 1.20. Warning 1.25 PM. Up Whitefoot Lane, two came over close and dropped. Near Northover one very close. I dived under a big tree, and 2 boys about 13 or 14 yrs also. To Mum. All Clear. 2.15 PM. 2 slices of boiled raisin pudding and cup of tea. Gave Mum letter that came for Dorrie. Away 2.45 P.M, to Farningham. To meet Vi 5.00 PM. Waited to see Irene 5.35 p m. Cup of tea and chips. Home 7.00 PM. Vi home 7.30 PM. Tea and bacon sandwiches. Alert 9.50 PM. 8-9 passed over here, and went off. All Clear 10.10 PM.

Saturday 29th July 1944

Up 6.00 AM. All Clear 6.50 AM. Depot 7.55 AM.

Took bunk fittings out, cleaned shelter, replaced bunks other side, tightened beds up; that gives us 6" more elbow room. Lay down after dinner. Some alerts after dinner. Pryor to Bancroft Rd. 4.15 P.M, at Stepney. Tyler, because Pryor had only 5 men, sent No. 2 with them, to make the number up. Only 9 men left at the depot, so he split them up to make 2 parties. Clary in charge of one. I, the other. Clary out to Redman's Road 7.00 PM. Pryor back at 8.00 P.M, approx., and they missed a bomb that fell in Burdett Rd by Lovat Arms. Pryor's gang shifted ton of stuff looking for a man whom nobody knew, and nobody was certain whether he was there or not. Clary's gang searching for a young girl, who was found to have been evacuated to Peterborough five days ago. This service gets more mishandled every day. We are first out tonight again. I believe Clary asks for that, but it is not fair to the other men. To the library with Wenzel, alert while we were there, so grabbed four books and came away.

Sunday 20th July 1944

Up 7.00 AM. Home 9.45 AM. Cleaned shelter out. Aired bedclothes, had fire going in shelter. As we sat down to dinner, warning went. On and off until evening. I managed to bath between bombs. Bed 10.20 PM. Brought Vi's shoes home. 4/-.

Monday 31st August 1944

Up 6.15 AM. All Clear. Depot 7.55 AM. Spent all morning making a rough armchair. Lay down after dinner. Alert about 2.30 PM. Bomb fell on Surrey side of the river, and Tyler called for Clary to take him and us to find out where it fell. I asked Tyler what the idea was. He said Jolly had given instructions to the effect that when a bomb fell somewhere near, we were to go and look for it. The fire service already do this. What about the light rescue? We were supposed to help them, and take over if it should be too heavy for them; but even so, they, and us, are supposed to wait for control to give the order. Now it looks as if everyone will congregate to a possible incident, while leaving an almost empty depot against a more probable certain incident, while we chase 'might be's'. Ridiculous. We did lots better during 1940-41, when the 'important people' were ready to fly to Canada, and let us stew; we certainly did a much better job. The control (or is it the Town Hall?), behave as if we were their own pet toy, to be put in motion at every slight scare. We drove to West Ferry Road, where a policeman instructed us, that the bomb had fallen over the river. Tyler 'was lost'. I told him to use the speaking tube. He grabbed it, from the pipe, and started to blow the whistle. I laughed, took the mouthpiece and whistle from him, fixed it back on the tube, called Clary, and told him to return: we did after getting to Garford St. After tea, snooker. After supper, to the Pin - shut. To the Tooke with Wenzel. Half pint, left in disgust. Pride, where we were treated the same. 31s until Alert about 11.30 PM. To bed.

HEAVY RESCUE SQUAD WORK ON THE ISLE OF DOGS

Tuesday 1st August 1944

Up 6.00 AM. All Clear. Warning 6.40 AM, and All Clear. Home 8.30 AM. Paid rent, went to Freemans. Brownhill Rd. Bought half a pound of liver. Alert 2.33 PM, so went to shelter, and slept until 4.30 PM. Cooked liver and bacon for tea. Did not sleep until warning went at 4.10 AM. Wednesday.

Wednesday 2nd August 1944

Up 6.00 AM. All clear. Alert 6.40, lasted 13 minutes. Out 7.20, Depot 7.43. In all morning. Out this afternoon. Clary. Samways, A.A. Crawley, and I, to Launch St, ostensibly to bring timber back, but in reality to enable Clary to get ironing-board, and a pair of steps, looted from F. & T. Thornes Joinery Works. He sold the steps to Bracken for 10/-. The timber we brought back was too rotten to burn. Shaved, after tea snooker. To the Pride, with Tuting. Forbes and Wenzel. Asked Clary if we were first out again. He said, "No." Told me he used to ask Knowlson, if he could always be out first. I am quite content to take my turn, and if he wanted to go out first, he could go, but not me.

Thursday 3rd August 1944

31s. Alert 11.20 PM. Very heavy tonight, slept intermittently. Awake 5.00 AM. Clary said Pryor had gone to Bow Rd, to L.C.C. Infirmary, and we would be going to relieve him. As we usually work 4 hour periods. I could not see how we could relieve him by the time we finish at 8.00 AM. All Clear 5.55 AM. Up 6.30. Alert 6.40 AM. Bomb fell at Tunnel Ave. Big fire broke out immediately. Stayed until All Clear about 9.00 AM. Bomb dropped at Matthew T. Shaw's, blasted the Nelson again, beside Chapel House Street and surroundings.

One outside the Wheatsheaf at Greenwich end of the subway. One in Blackheath Hill, one near St. Johns Hospital, which is well blasted. Alert as I got to Brownhill Rd. In shelter at Canadian Ave. Home 10.30 AM. All Clear 11.40 AM. Dinner at Meals Centre. 12.20 PM. Alert. Back home to shelter, slept until 2.30 PM. All Clear. Sat in sun all afternoon until 5.30 PM. Prepared tea 6.10

PM. Salmon. Sat in garden to tea, when Vi came home 6.10 PM. Sunning myself again until 8.30 PM. Heavy gunfire could be heard at times in the distance. Letter from Mum at Somerset.

One from Percy Freeman, to get bicycle. £2.15.2. Filled in form yesterday, for tea, sugar, and milk. Kiddell gave me authorization papers this morning. One and three quarter pounds of tea, 2lbs sugar. 16 pints milk.

Friday 4th August 1944

Up 6.00 AM. All Clear. Alert 6.30 to 6.40. Depot 7.50 AM. Got authorization form for tea, sugar, milk. Took one and a quarter pounds of tea for myself. Alerts on and off. Laid in sun. To the library, after tea. To the Pin. Skittles until 11.00 PM.

Saturday 5th August 1944

Up 6.30 Alert and All Clear. Home 8.30. Gave Vi tea in shelter, and jam sponge. To Brownhill Rd to get cycle. Picked up parcel at Catford, that the kids had sent, gooseberries had all gone rotten. Salvaged the kids' letter. To the butcher, and greengrocers. Read, and lay about in the sun all day.

Sunday 6th August 1944

Up 6.50 AM. Tea in bed in shelter. Depot 8.50 AM.

Alerts on and off. This afternoon, one dropped in Galbraith St - Strattondale St. Lewington went to it, came back 10 minutes later, and had to go back with Tyler, as he had not taken incident note with him. Tyler is truly incompetent. Another immediately after this, in the South Dock, in the water, holed ship. 1 injured. This one nearly caught Tyler on his way back. Soon after, we to Galbraith St. Launch St, and Chapel in Glengall Grove, to remove dangerous structures. Did not do St. John's Church or the Chapel.

Pint in the London[1]. Back, and out again with Pryor to Manchester Rd (332). I cleared roof. Ginsburg too scared. Back to depot. To the Pin. Skittles at 10.30. Made tea about 11.00 PM. Alert soon after. Bed 11.30 PM. (Vi spent day in St. James Park).

London Tavern after being damaged by bombing[2]

Monday 7th August 1944

Up 6.40 AM. Tea already made. Home 8.30 AM. Lay about in the garden all day. Had tea in the garden. Osford gave us some runner beans for dinner. To the King Alfred. No beer. Bed 10.30 PM. Alert about 11.30. Charlie came in time for breakfast, went soon after.

Tuesday 8th August 1944

Up 6.00 AM. All Clear. Warning 6.40, All Clear 6.55. Depot 7.55 AM. Tyler came in, prepared to put everyone to work. Got

---

[1] London Tavern, 393 Manchester Rd.
[2] Photo: Island History Trust Collection

Samways, Lewington, Wenzel, to take hardcore used to cover shelter, away, as it looked untidy, and put it on the mortuary shelter, which the mortuary men have not yet covered. Loafed about all morning in the sun.

After dinner lay in the sun reading, made tea 3.30 PM. To the library after tea. Snooker, made tea after 10.00 PM. This morning, during short alert, bomb fell on foreshore at Morton's. Manchester Rd. (Badcock's.) 5 injured, invasion barge smashed. Even now. Tyler and Co don't know the Island.

Wednesday 9th August 1944

Up 6.00 AM. All Clear. Alert 7.00 AM. All Clear 7.20 AM. Home 8.45 AM. Stayed in garden all morning. This afternoon to Catford, loaf, sausages. Got tea ready. 6.00 PM. Sausages, tomatoes. Read this evening. Bed 11.00 PM.

Thursday 10th August 1944

Up 6.15 AM. Depot 7.45 AM. Clary absent. In all day. After dinner Hawkins gave me £2 towards cycle. To the library. Bridge on the way back, and Alert. Snooker after tea. To the Blacksmiths with Forbes and Wenzel. Bed 11.00 PM. (Raffled half a pound of tea, got 6/- for it, and put half a pound away to take home).

Friday 11th August 1944

Up 6.00 AM. All Clear. Alert 6.30 AM. All clear 7.05 AM. Home 9.00 AM. Letters from Mrs. Harris and the kids'. Stayed home all day. Drove seat pillar in cycle, and have made a mess of it. Lay in the garden this afternoon. Read this evening. To bed 11.30 PM. (Brought half a pound of tea home.)

Saturday 12th August 1944

Up 6.15 AM. Depot 7.40 AM. Hawkins gave me another £2 for bicycle. Out to Chapel House Street. Nobody knew where it was. Salvage provision. I jabbed Clary in the left eye with a piece of wood. Bought half a pound of tomatoes. Back to depot 11.15 AM. Clary to St. Andrews Hospital. Came back with his eye in a sling.

Snooker this evening. To the Pin with Tuting. Forbes and Wenzel. Pryor came in later, back to skittles. Tea 11.00 p.m. Alert and to bed 11.10 p.m.

(Washed out billiard room, canteen and sleeping quarters. Paid milkman 4/5.)

Sunday 13th August 1944

Up 6.50 AM. All Clear. Alert 7.45 AM. All Clear 8.20 AM. Home 9.30 AM. Breakfast. Pulled all cabbages up, and beans. Dinner, lay down this afternoon. Read all evening. Wrote to Doncaster. Bed at 10.20 PM.

Monday 14th August 1944

Up at 6.00 AM. All Clear. Alert 6.45 AM. All Clear 7.00 AM. Depot 7.40 AM. Loafed about all morning. This afternoon, Pryor's gang, with Tyler, to Preston's Rd. Came back, went out again immediately, found they had done a job at Cotton St by mistake. Imagine going out, not knowing where the job is! Back again – out again. (Well, Well!) Skittles this evening. To the Pin. More skittles. Took 8/10d from the table. Tea 3/5d. Bed 11.30. Up 2.30 AM. Big bomb came over nearly scraping roof-tops. E. to W. Back to bed. (Rusby gave pint of milk to Hawkins for cat. He'll pay for it, too. Wenzel and Bracken not here today also Carlile. Brought half a pound of tea to depot to raffle. 1lb of sugar for club.

Tuesday 15th August 1944

Up 6.40 AM. Home 8.45 AM. Alert 9.10 AM. Took cycle to Parks, had to leave it. Home 1.05 p.m. Alerts this afternoon. Vi home 6.15 p.m. Another alert 6.45 p.m. Letters from Mum and Doncaster, came yesterday.

Bill Regan in A.R.P. uniform, in a photo sent to Vi at Christmas 1944

POSTSCRIPT

Bill's interest in photography continued well after the end of World War II. In the late 1980s, he wandered around the Island and took photos of some of his old haunts, just a few of which are included here.

The Pier Tavern. The Regan's home at 171 Manchester Rd was located at the leftmost end of the 1960s flats to the left of the pub.

The former road entrance to the Mudchute anti-aircraft gun installation, now part of a city farm. Bill's shadow can be seen.

Preston's Rd just south of the swing bridge. The place that Bill and Vi had to take shelter from bombing in the night of 30th/31st December 1940.

The former Newcastle Arms. Photo taken from Saunders Ness Rd, location of Cubitt Town School during WWII.

HEAVY RESCUE SQUAD WORK ON THE ISLE OF DOGS

Ann at the start of an Island Carnival in Glengall Grove, outside the George, 1986.

Bill and Vi celebrated their Diamond Wedding Anniversary in 1991:

Joan (middle) with Bill and Vi at their Diamond Wedding Anniversary celebration.

Sadly, Bill passed away a couple of years later, in 1993 at the age of 84. Vi died in 1997 at the age of 85.